THE ESSENTIAL

WILDERNESS NAVIGATOR

SECOND
EDITION

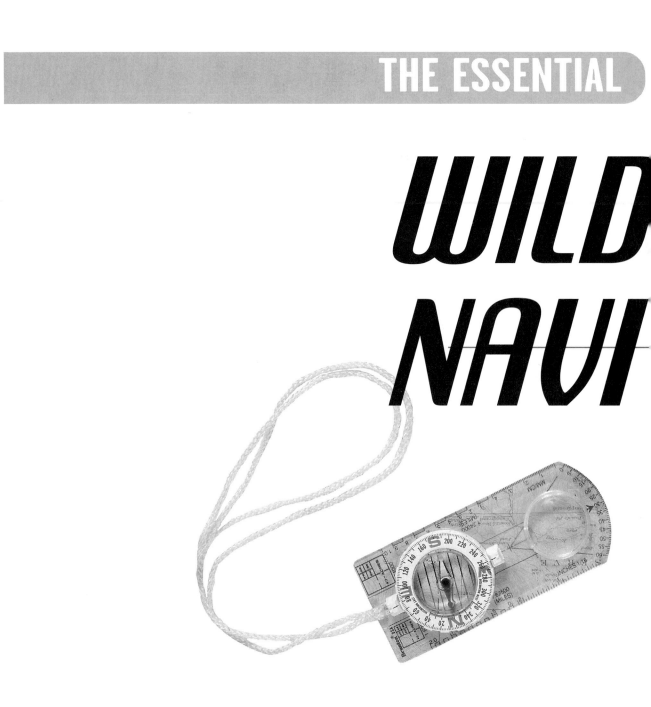

THE ESSENTIAL

WILD

NAVI

ERNESS
GATOR

SECOND EDITION

DAVID SEIDMAN
with PAUL CLEVELAND

Illustrations by Christine Erikson

RAGGED MOUNTAIN PRESS / McGRAW-HILL

CAMDEN, MAINE • NEW YORK • SAN FRANCISCO • WASHINGTON, D.C. • AUCKLAND
BOGOTÁ • CARACAS • LISBON • LONDON • MADRID • MEXICO CITY • MILAN
MONTREAL • NEW DELHI • SAN JUAN • SINGAPORE • SYDNEY • TOKYO • TORONTO

ALSO IN THE RAGGED MOUNTAIN PRESS ESSENTIAL SERIES

The Essential Backpacker: A Complete Guide for the Foot Traveler, Adrienne Hall

The Essential Cross-Country Skier: A Step-by-Step Guide, Paul Petersen
and Richard A. Lovett

The Essential Outdoor Gear Manual: Equipment Care, Repair, and Selection,
2nd edition, Annie Getchell and Dave Getchell Jr.

The Essential Sea Kayaker: A Complete Guide for the Open-Water Paddler,
2nd edition, David Seidman

The Essential Snowshoer: A Step-by-Step Guide, Marianne Zwosta

The Essential Touring Cyclist: A Complete Guide for the Bicycle Traveler, 2nd edition,
Richard A. Lovett

The Essential Whitewater Kayaker: A Complete Course, Jeff Bennett

Ragged Mountain Press
A Division of The McGraw-Hill Companies

10 9 8 7 6 5
Copyright © 1995, 2001 Ragged Mountain Press

Library of Congress Cataloging-in-Publication Data
Seidman, David.
    The essential wilderness navigator / David Seidman, with Paul Cleveland : illustrations by
  Christine Erikson.
        p.   cm.
    Includes bibliographical references and index.
    ISBN 0-07-136110-3 (alk. paper)
    1. Wilderness survival. 2. Orientation. I. Paul, Cleveland. II. Title.
  GV200.5.S44 2000
  796.58—dc21   00-024811

Questions regarding the content of this book should be addressed to
Ragged Mountain Press
P.O. Box 220
Camden, ME 04843
www.raggedmountainpress.com

Questions regarding the ordering of this book should be addressed to
The McGraw-Hill Companies
Customer Service Department
P.O. Box 547
Blacklick, OH 43004
Retail customers: 1-800-262-4729
Bookstores: 1-800-722-4726

This book is printed on 70# Citation at R.R. Donnelley; Design by Dede Cummings; Production management by Janet Robbins; Page layout by Deborah Evans; Edited by Tom McCarthy and Constance Burt; photos on pages 68–73 by Jeff Slack, Classic Photography; photos on page 146 courtesy Garmin.

CONTENTS

INTRODUCTION

This book is for all outdoorspeople, and for those who *would* be outdoorspeople were it not for the fear of getting lost. Staying found is not an instinct or an innate skill; like riding a bicycle or mastering municipal bus routes, it can be learned.

Indeed, the basics can be learned quite quickly, and most outdoorspeople are content with that. But the more time we spend outdoors, and the more adventurous we become, the greater the chances of encountering a situation that baffles our orienteering skills. It could be a trick of the weather, a few minutes' inattention, a decision to cut across country to a visible destination rather than following the trail—and suddenly panic is rising as you're forced to admit to yourself that you don't know where you are.

This book explains how to stay out of those situations, and what to do when you *do* get lost. It has been laid out in a progressive format. You start here, go to there, and then finally wind up where you want to be. Once you've learned something, you use it as a steppingstone to other knowledge. As ideas accumulate, you'll be surprised how far you've progressed. It will all be done in small doses. It will be easy to head back if you think you're not yet fully in the picture—which is how you should explore any unknown area.

Chapter 1 provides basic training for perceiving the environment. No one is born with a sixth sense. What passes for it is the learned ability to observe—to see, smell, hear, and sense details in the world through which you pass. You have to learn all this, and we show you how. This chapter contains the most important sentence in the book: *If you plan to return along the same route, turn around frequently to see what your path will look like on the way back.*

In chapter 2 we take the next step, to learn

what cannot be sensed. We do this with maps, which are the most effective way of portraying parts of the world beyond our vision. Of course, you could also use the written word, but think how cumbersome it would be to describe even the smallest patch of land in sufficient detail to allow strangers to find their way. If a picture is worth a thousand words, then a map is a complete guidebook. But it is a guidebook written in its own language, a language we show you how to interpret. Once you can do this, the world is in your hands.

Next we give you a point of reference that can be used anywhere on the planet and a gadget that always shows where it is. This gadget, as you might have guessed, is a compass. It gives wayfinding insurance and, once you know its tricks, provides the ultimate in dependability. As you'll see, it is a guiding finger that does a lot more than point north.

Next, you'll put it all together. Taking your newfound sense of direction and ability to read a map and use a compass, you can start to navigate. And as you practice, you'll learn when you can relax precision for the sake of convenience and speed. You'll discover that, in practice, land navigation consists for the most part of orienting off surrounding landmarks such as distant peaks, river drainages, or slope aspects and angles. The compass is used mostly to orient the map to these landmarks, and then for rough intermediate bearings that help you field-check that you're following the appropriate "line of least resistance" in the desired direction.

As time goes by, you'll find most often that you just travel with map in hand, keeping up with passing landmarks, rather than plotting and following exact directional vectors. Vegetation, obstacles, and game trails (which can be followed quickly) will all divert you somewhat from your plotted bearings. Seldom will you stick to tight courses or make square, equal-sided detours around obstacles as this book sets forth. But we walk before we run, and it is good to learn map-and-compass navigation as a discipline before you practice it as an art.

In chapter 6, we move beyond map and compass use to examine some of the signs that can be found in nature. Chapter 7 touches lightly on specialized navigation for extreme environments. Neither chapter pretends to be thorough, but they show you further directions to explore.

And exploration is what this book is about.

Bon voyage!

WHAT'S NEW IN THIS EDITION

The navigational skills taught in this book are timeless, so why are we publishing a second edition?

Technological changes and competition in the marketplace have pushed GPS units out of the expensive-toy category and into the affordable mainstream of wilderness navigation. When the first edition was published in 1995, a global positioning system (GPS) receiver was an expensive novelty; now you can find units no bigger than a TV remote for around $100. To keep pace with these changes, we added a chapter on the basics of GPS navigation and CD-ROM maps. May this new information keep you from wandering off in a state of bewilderment in the electronic wilderness.

We also added a new full-color section that enhances the discussion on translating the language of maps by explaining how to read the "codes" embedded in topographic maps. With the ease of quick reference, a beginning map-reader can develop a strong and clear understanding of what these symbols mean in real life—on the ground, so to speak.

With more than a decade as a freelance writer for publications such as *Backpacker*, *Climbing*, and *Summit* magazines, guiding whitewater rafting trips, and teaching Outward Bound novices the rudiments of navigation, I've often turned to this book for its clear and concise explanations. In teaching and in writing, as in wilderness navigation, simplicity works best.

Paul J. Cleveland

1 A SENSE OF DIRECTION

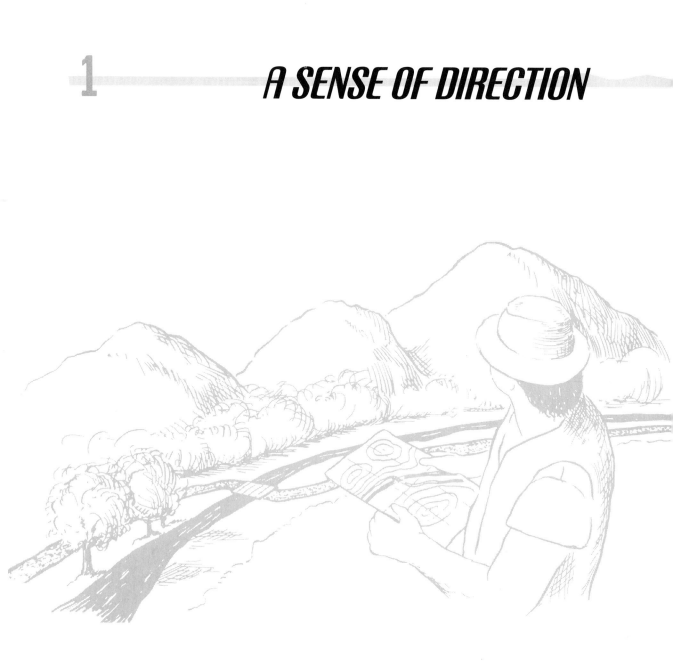

This is the most important chapter in the book and also the most challenging. All that follows is about specialized techniques, presented in cookbook style—straightforward methods that anyone can learn. However, the contents of this chapter are not so clear-cut and cannot be presented in such a direct manner.

The next few pages explore the mindset of the navigator—a way of looking at your environment and sensing the clues around you. This helps you make better use of the techniques you'll learn later and, ultimately, even liberate you from them.

Primarily, this chapter is about judgment—a way of bringing all your senses to bear on the bigger problem. Good judgment is no less present in the art of getting around without getting lost—more often known as navigating—than in other fields of endeavor. Technique is fine and necessary, but it's a foundation of good, informed judgment that keeps you out of trouble.

That range, too, ran into the northwest, becoming fainter and finally vanishing into the dim blue distance; it ran parallel with the granite range, and it had to be the Yukon–Northwest Territories divide. Divide to what?, I wondered, peering through the glass—for neither of these ranges was marked on the map, and the map itself was a beautiful blank with the Flat River represented by a dotted line in the wrong place. That was the charm of that map: one might chance upon almost anything in those empty, uncrowded spaces.

—R. M. Patterson, *Dangerous River*

Luckily for us, as in other fields, this judgment is not inherited; it can be learned. To become a proficient navigator, you don't need the genes of a Vasco da Gama or a Daniel Boone (who claimed never to get lost, although he had on occasion been *bewildered* for several days at a time). Nor is this judgment a mystical power, such as European explorers once attributed to "primitive natives." To be sure, there seemed to be extrasensory ability involved, but it was only the hard work of people trying to survive. They were great wayfinders, but they had to practice all their lives to achieve that ability.

To help you on your way, here's the foundation stone of all wayfinding and the essential key to not getting lost: Watch Where You Are Going.

Perhaps this sounds like an oversimplification. Maybe, but that's what makes it so beautiful. There are no complicated theorems and nothing to memorize. Just stay in touch with the world through which you walk. Be aware of details and your chances of getting where you want to go, and back, are pretty good.

Sometimes the difficult part is knowing exactly *which* details to be aware of. But you can learn that, too—you'll find them all in the pages of this book.

So begin here. Before you jump ahead to the more-or-less mechanical techniques that look like quick-fix solutions, build the foundation of good judgment—that not-so-common sixth sense.

LOCATING YOUR SIXTH SENSE

We'd like to be able to encourage you with the good news that all of us have hidden deep within us an innate ability to find our way, that during evolution we were left with some spare parts from the homing pigeon. But we haven't and weren't. Or, at least, that is the way conservative, rigorous researchers in this field see things.

Others, however, remain unconvinced, and every once in a while they come up with some rather promising (or at least entertaining) theories. My favorite is the revelation that we really can follow our noses. Scientists have discovered that we all have traces of iron in our noses located in the ethmoid bone (the one between the eyes). Some suggest that these trace deposits help us find direction relative to the earth's magnetic field.

A researcher at the University of Manchester, in England, found that when magnets were placed on the right side of a person's head, the subject tended to veer, by an obvious amount, to the right. Magnets on the left side drew the subject to the left. This proved, or so the researchers claimed, that we are affected by magnetic fields. Many other animals, such as dolphins, tuna, sea turtles, salamanders, and bees, have similar magnetic deposits near their brains, perhaps to help them navigate their way through life. There are also certain single-celled organisms that always swim toward the northern side of a test dish.

The ability to sense direction became a minor scientific obsession in the mid-1800s. In 1873, a respected journal invited contributions on the topic, getting responses from such luminaries as Charles Darwin. The contributors agreed that man and animals probably made use of some instinctive direction-finding ability. None could cite any verifiable evidence, however. Instead, they used phrases like "guided by a kind of unerring instinct."

During the same period, medical science for the first time delved into the world of the blind, making it an active area of research. Of great fascination was the ability of blind people to avoid obstacles while finding their way. It was thought that the loss of one sense might enhance the others, or that it might bring forth the presence of a completely new one. Of the many studies performed, one done in 1905 by Émile Javal referred to the sixth sense. Javal was convinced that this sense was similar to our tactile sensations, except that rather than physical contact with an object, it required the projection of "ether waves."

While this may sound strange to modern ears, Javal's theory was tame compared with those of some of his contemporaries, who went completely otherworldly and mystical in their explanations. In all fairness, though, it is a baffling phenomenon. Lest we judge these experimenters too harshly, we should consider how many of us, when watching a blind person wend his or her way, find it hard not to believe that something inexplicable is occurring.

It is true that many blind people can perceive the presence of large objects and judge their distance from them with a surprising degree of accuracy. They do this by becoming more attuned to the differences in sound as it bounces back from their surroundings with a rudimentary form of echolocation. No instinctive powers are brought forth, no ether waves—just highly developed, highly trained natural senses.

To date, science has shown no evidence of a naturally occurring sixth sense of direction. Yet, we still want to believe that it exists. We all know at least one person who never seems to get lost. It seems that there should be some explanation for this.

Probably the most pervasive, and persuasive, arguments are leftovers from the era of European exploration and colonization. Adventurers took home stories of so-called primitives who could navigate through dense forests or over featureless seas with no mechanical aids. The peculiar thing is that the tales about these great native trackers became more frequent as the European explorers became increasingly dependent on technology. Ancient writings in the East and West make no mention of any extraordinary ability to navigate; perhaps it was taken for granted. But, as European civilization removed itself farther and farther from nature, the more astounding those feats appeared. It was a sign of awareness that an old world was disappearing and with it, perhaps, old navigational skills.

By 1768, Captain James Cook, one of history's great navigators, had at his disposal the sextant for calculating latitude, a dependable chronometer to find longitude, astronomical tables, the best charts of the time, and a good working knowledge of how the earth was laid out. On a map of the world, he could accurately place himself within a few miles, no matter where he was. The system he used (which, in principle, is the same used by modern navigators) was an abstract way of defining a position. It is based on locating yourself on an artificial grid made up of lines of latitude and longitude. The system works quite well, especially for those not familiar with the part of the world in which they find themselves. It worked so well that Cook—and most others of his time—began to think it was the only way to navigate.

Know Where You Go

Handing out whistles at the start of any Outward Bound course and telling students they need to wear them at all times always gets some laughs. "Whadda we need these for?" at least one student inevitably asks. "You'll need it when you wander away during a late-night nature call and you can't find your way back to camp" is my usual reply. This prompts a few more laughs.

Here's a real-life case, which points up the need to be aware of your surroundings at all times, even when you think you're just a few steps away from the comforts of camp.

It was the end of a long, stormy day. We had picked a choice campsite near a place called West Oval Lake in Washington's Lake Chelan–Sawtooth Wilderness. Nearby was an old privy. After dinner, things wound down and students prepared to retire for the evening. Conversations carried on quietly as I noticed one of the students, we'll call her Jane, headed over to the privy for a last visit before bedtime.

Some time later, just before turning in myself, I did a final check on the students. "Nope, Jane's still gone to the bathroom," one of her tarpmates commented when I asked. I tried to recall when I saw her heading out. Too long, I realized. I hastily grabbed my co-instructor for a search, telling the remaining students to stay put while we went to look for Jane.

We crossed the 50 yards from camp over to the privy, but found it empty. From there, we continued away from camp, traversing steep cliffy slopes in the dark. Ten minutes later we located a whistle-blowing and a very embarrassed Jane in a nasty place. Her embarrassment sprang not so much from getting lost but because she had laughed about having to wear the whistle. How had Jane ended up so far from camp? She hadn't paid attention to the bearing back and had headed off in the wrong direction. From there, she began second-guessing her gut feeling and sense of direction. Big—and very common—mistake.

PJC

So it can be understood with what wonder the captain beheld his Polynesian guides. How, he thought, could these islanders find tiny atolls hundreds of miles across a trackless ocean with none of his fine gear and knowledge? The only explanation was that these "children of nature" still possessed a special sense that civilized man had lost long ago. It was an attractive and romantic theme, and it got great play back home.

In truth, the guides he encountered had their own, equally valid, system of navigation. Theirs was a more direct way of defining a position, accomplished through intimate experience rather than abstract thought.

In their system, you start from any known position and travel a certain distance in a set direction. If you know how far away something is and in what direction it lies, you know where it is relative to you. In Cook's system, a position was absolute; in their system, a position was always relative. Accumulate enough of these directions and distances and you can define the world and your position in it. There were no secret or extra senses, just repeated travels and a great awareness of the world in which they lived.

What seemed like a sixth sense to the Europeans was only an ability to discern direction and distance. For direction, Polynesian navigators used the heavens, winds, waves, plants, and a whole guidebook full of subtle but learnable signs. For calculating distance, they had to look within themselves.

To many people of the world, distance is flexible. The Polynesians had no word for *distance* as such. They used time—the time it took to get somewhere. That was less abstract and easier to comprehend.

In practical terms, of course, it makes no difference how you measure it. Defining a distance as 20 miles can be just as useful as saying it's a two-day walk. But time is sometimes a handier way to express distance because we all have a natural sense of rhythm. We sense time with an internal rhythm or pulse, and it is the one "extra" sense that has been substantiated. Humans are just one of many species having a sense of the passage of time. A bee, for instance, not only knows its travel times, but also can share this information with other bees. Many of us can tell the time with fair accuracy without looking at our watches, or estimate how long we have been at a job. It's a good, built-in measuring system, though it can be distorted by fatigue, heightened physical effort, or low blood sugar.

Cook and his Polynesian guides were equally good navigators. Each had a system that worked well. Yet the Europeans, out of conceit, refused to believe that others might have a knowledge equal to their own. So they attributed it to primal instincts, something that came before knowledge. From this arrogance and misunderstanding sprang the myth of a sense of direction.

Now, after centuries of experience, we can learn from both systems of navigation. Later in this book, we will navigate by both Cook's abstract (i.e., absolute) positioning and his guides' direct (i.e., relative) positioning. As you might imagine, there are advantages and disadvantages to both.

What has passed for a sense of direction is nothing more than careful observation and accumulated knowledge, of which we are all capable. Explorers were astounded by the memories of the Pacific Islanders, Australian aborigines, and the Indians of North America for the smallest details of a landscape. While we might have the same capability, modern life does not encourage it. Because these traits aren't needed to survive, they are not taught or passed on. Yet, we can still tune in to this way of thinking and learn to see.

We can also learn to open up our other senses. With some concentration, you can tap into and become aware of sounds and smells, as well as what can be seen. While most of our information for direction finding is gathered by sight, studies show that smells and sounds also can be useful. Smells, in particular, imprint themselves in our memories. Some people claim that smell is the most sensitive sense, and the last to leave us in death. So open your ears and nose, as well as your eyes, when observing landmarks on the trail.

We all have the ability to remember these details and apply them to finding our way, although some people seem better able to do so than others. One person might remember routes previously traveled by relying on specific landmarks. In driving to a friend's house, he would turn left at the

. . . believing this to be an essential point in the geography of this western part of the Continent I determined to remain at all events untill I obtained the necessary data for fixing it's [sic] latitude. Longitude &c.

—Meriwether Lewis,
The Journals of Lewis and Clark

faded blue building, right at the park with broken swings, and left at the dry cleaners. Someone else might use a different method, keeping track of how long she's traveled and in what direction. To get to that same friend's house, she might use her internal clock to drive in one direction for 3 minutes, turn left, go a short distance at 40 miles an hour, turn right, and then drive for 30 seconds before making a final left turn.

Neither system is superior, and neither group gets lost more often than the other. There are different ways of navigating, and very often there is an overlapping of the two methods. The fact that the latter group does not rely on external signals might be a reason why some people are loath to admit they are lost or to ask directions. To their senses, at least, they are right on track with no clues to tell them otherwise—they have no reason to feel lost.

The former group's affinity for distinct landmarks may be the reason some people have trouble reading maps. Because they respond better to complicated chains of landmarks and not to distances and direction (i.e., the defining parameters of a map), they may be at a disadvantage when the only navigational help is a map. Or maybe it's just that some people are less likely to be exposed to map-reading when young. Certainly anyone can become an expert map-reader.

The hormones in your brain dictate the way you navigate and the techniques that work best for you. Those hormones affect the way we experience the world and the way we compile our mental maps (we say more about mental mapping later). So when you begin your studies on finding your way, think about how you remember where you are going. If you favor one method over another, use it.

Regardless of chemistry, we all acquire our wayfinding skills gradually. The great Polynesian navigators started their educations as small children. Even with all the information in this book, it takes time to develop your abilities and to sense what is out there—it can't be rushed. So enjoy the experience of getting disoriented every once in a while, and the pleasure of finding your way back.

A good way to start feeling your way around a new environment is to follow the example of most wandering tribespeople. They get their sense of direction in small doses, exploring the world around them a little at a time. This has often been referred to as a *home-based system*, using home as a constant point of reference. From their villages, they continually wander out and back. Each trip is a little longer and in alternating directions. As they travel, they gather details for their ever-expanding mental maps, piecing together a complex image of their world. Because they always maintain a mental link to their home base, they rarely get lost.

This type of wayfinding-by-exploration is reassuring in that there is always a connection to where you started. Security comes from its thread of continuity, which is why it is also known as the "Principle of Ariadne's Thread." In Greek mythology, Ariadne gave her lover, Theseus, a ball of thread to unwind as he entered the Minotaur's labyrinth. After killing the beast, he escaped by following the thread. Hansel and Gretel's trail of bread crumbs was a similar method—one also reputedly used by the Indians of British Columbia who, when conditions were right, dropped cedar chips in the wakes of their canoes to mark the way home in thick fog.

It is only the scholar who appreciates that all history consists of successive excursions from a single starting-point, to which man returns again and again to organize yet another search for a durable scale of values.

—Aldo Leopold,
A Sand County Almanac

He reached the summit of the plateau beyond Comb Wash, left the old road and headed south, guiding himself by the stars. The going was rough, rocky, over a highly irregular surface cut up by draws, gullies, and ravines, some of them tending west, others east back to Comb Wash. Hayduke tried to follow the divide between the two drainage systems—not easy in the dark, in a piece of backcountry where he had never set foot before.

—Edward Abbey,
The Monkey Wrench Gang

The problem with the home-based system is that you can't just show up at an unfamiliar location and begin to find your way around. However, it can be adapted to serve this purpose. Instead of home, you relate all directions to any prominent local feature, or *landmark*. This feature can be a central point, such as a building or a mountain, or a long line, like a river or a road. Using your chosen reference point or line to make a mental map brings you very close to thinking and finding your way like those "primitives" with their magical sense of direction.

These techniques emphasize an important point: you need to use something other than yourself as a reference. A good way to get lost is to relate to the world in terms of yourself: "That mountain is to my left, the river is behind me." As you move through the world, the position of these objects changes relative to you. It's easy to get confused and then lost. A better way is to think on a grander scale. Look for a constant reference that never moves and keep relating back to it. We've already done this with a home base or a local feature, and you'll discover many other ways in the following chapters.

This ability to experience your environment from a *geocentric perspective* (i.e., your position relative to the world) rather than an *egocentric perspective* (i.e., the world's position relative to you) is a step in the right direction. Practiced on a regular basis, it can even keep you from getting disoriented. For example, in one case study, a young man never seemed to make any deliberate efforts to orient himself and yet rarely got lost in a strange city. The explanation came from his early training. For some reason, his mother had always given him directions using the points of the compass, rather than the more usual left or right. She would say, "Get me the brush on the north [instead of right] side of the dresser," or "sit in the chair on the east side of the porch." Eventually, the young man developed an unusual ability to move in a complicated path for relatively long periods and retain his orientation without paying attention to it. He saw himself as moving within the world, he didn't perceive the world to be moving around him. In this way, he always remained properly oriented.

Long ago, the state of being oriented meant to face the east, toward the rising sun (hence, the origin of the word *Orient*). You aligned yourself with everything else through that one constant direction. We now use north (and south) for orienting because it is more convenient to find north from the stars or with a compass. Like the young man in the previous example, as long as you can stay aligned with some external reference, it is easier to keep track of where you are.

Although we have no innate sense of direction, we can develop the ability to stay oriented. Practice is essential. Use what you feel comfortable with and what comes naturally. Try to combine observed landmarks, memorable details, direction and distance covered, and points or lines of reference. Practice every day, no matter where you are.

HOW NOT TO GET LOST

You'll find that it won't take long before you, too, can locate what passes convincingly for a genuine sense of direction. In the previous section, we discovered that while we are not born with a sense of direction, it can be acquired. By learning to stay aware of our surroundings and by maintaining a reference to some constant, we should be able to avoid getting lost. We also alluded to the fact that there are some simple ways to do this. Here they are.

Bear in mind that there is no one correct technique for finding your way; the proper method is to use all methods. Employ what is at hand, what you feel sure about. During an outing, opportunities arise to use a variety of skills. The more you know, the better off you'll be and the less anxious about getting lost. Learn when you can, practice what you learn, and use it all.

Here's an example of what I mean. Two friends making a cross-country flight in a small plane had very different personalities and ways of keeping track of where they were. One loved gadgets. She had all sorts of electronic gear that told her where she was and where she was going. She never had to look out the window. Her partner had the opposite approach. He looked for landmarks, kept track of time and distance, observed the sun and wind, and ignored the instruments. At a given time, both agreed to point on the map to where they thought they were. When the time came, they were both right.

They were also both wrong. A better way to avoid getting lost would have been to use *everything* they had. Watch the electronics, look at the landscape, monitor the compass, and read the map. This way, if one system fails or seems questionable, you have backups. This also allows you to evaluate your judgment objectively by comparing information from various sources. In navigation, you can never have too much information.

The technical methods of finding your way with map and compass are explained later in this book. All you will need for those chapters is some inexpensive gear and some practice using it. For now, though, let's build up your basic wayfinding skills so you can make the kind of educated judgments that form the foundation of a dependable sense of direction.

The need for these basic skills begins even before you take your first step in the wilderness. When you find yourself entering a situation in which you might get lost—such as starting a hike (or arriving in a new city or walking into a shopping mall)—go no farther until you have picked out an easily identifiable feature that can be used as a reference. This can be a single point, such as a mountain, or a line, like a coast, river, or road. It can be something that is always visible to you as you travel or something whose existence is known only from a map. Without delay, locate yourself in terms of direction and distance to this reference. Now you know where your starting point is and your journey can begin. Your job is to keep track of your reference and where you are relative to it.

If the reference is a point, your routes radiate from it, spiral around it, or vector past it. If it is a line, think of it as a tree with branches leading out from and back to a central trunk, or with vines hanging parallel to the trunk.

A line is the handier of the two references because it lets you set up crossing lines (i.e., the tree's branches), giving you four primary directions. When using a compass, the main reference line is the north–south axis, from which you also get a perpendicular east–west line. You can do the same with any other reference line, such as a river, a range of hills, a coastline, a logging road, or a valley.

In a city, you might use a street as your main reference line. New York has Fifth Avenue, a main artery that runs the length of the city. This then becomes your uptown/downtown reference line,

from which you also get crosstown lines perpendicular to it.

Repeating patterns offer another type of reference line. These can be used in place of one central line, or for keeping yourself on course when not in sight of your main reference. A pattern could be any series of features, such as a series of rivers running parallel—or roughly so—to your main reference line. Or it could be streams (or streets) running into your reference line. For instance, most mountain ranges in the United States run north and south; the streams running from them usually trend east and west. Smaller patterns can be found in the way snow or sand drifts with the prevailing wind. Patterns are everywhere—use them.

Animals use naturally occurring reference lines, and so can you. Wildebeests follow ridges and rivers. Caribou travel along valleys or tree lines. Lemmings cross ice-covered lakes by keeping mountains to one side. And pigeons use the sun's shadow (i.e., a line) for orientation. You should try the same.

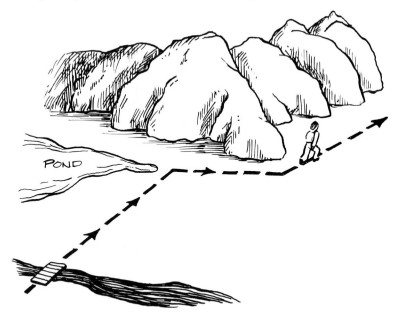

Repeating patterns. This hiker knows that the streams along her route run generally west to east and the hills trend south and north, so she is heading generally north. Every so often, she compares her map with the surrounding view, locating landmarks and checking her position. She glances at her compass when necessary. Although her approach seems casual, she knows where she is at all times through attention to the landscape.

When traveling toward a goal, as from a cabin to a lake, decide on a route and try to stick to it. If midcourse corrections are necessary, make them deliberate, definite, and retraceable. This way, even if you can't find the lake, you'll at least be able to retrace your steps to the cabin. If you just go out there and wander aimlessly, you might miss the lake *and* the cabin.

A lake is a good target to aim for because it's big. In contrast, a campsite by the lake would be a poor target, for it is relatively small and, therefore, harder to find. If you aimed for the campsite, how would you know in which direction to turn if you missed it? You wouldn't. But if you aimed for the lake, or a part of it (e.g., "the end nearest the hills"), you'd no doubt hit it. Then all you'd have to do is follow the shoreline toward the camp. To avoid getting lost, aim at a big target. Don't go for a hole in one—just get to the green and putt your way home from there.

When you intend to wander about rather than strike off toward a specific goal, you won't be able to stick to a set route. For this type of traveling, an easily recognizable reference is even more important, because it's all you'll have. You can use either a point or a line. With a point, head out and back over ever-increasing distances, gathering information and improving your knowledge of the area on each excursion. Or, if the point is always visible, like a tall mountain or building, you can wander as you will—as long as it stays in sight, you're OK. When you're working with a line, stay to one side of it while walking in a direction that is generally parallel to it. For example, wander about on one side of a river (or road), always heading upstream (or up-town). When you've had enough, return to the line and follow it downstream (or downtown) to where you started.

While underway, think of what you and the world around you looks like to a bird overhead. Envision the larger picture and your place in it. This is your mental map. Do this by continually updating your position through the use of sequential landmarks, or by keeping track of how far and in what directions you have gone.

Experiment with your internal rhythm, your natural ability to judge time (which is as useful in navigation as is distance traveled). Experiments show that many animals can measure time to an accuracy of 0.3 percent. In other words, they would be no more than 3 minutes off after a period of 16 hours and 40 minutes.

Humans do not have such extraordinary accuracy. However, with practice, we can come to within 10 minutes (although not consistently) in 12 hours—which is good enough in a pinch. Sharpen your skills at estimating time by trying to guess what time it is or how long you have been doing something. By all means, take your watch with you on the trail, but tune in your innate sense of time as you tune in your other senses.

Above all, stay aware of the world you are moving through. Every once in a while, turn off the radio in the car or stop talking on the trail. Watch where you are going, don't just follow the boots ahead of you. Look around constantly.

A good trick is to try to remember important features by their shape rather than color. Our brains retain forms better than hues and tones. But don't just depend on what you see; use all five senses, combining them into a sixth.

Use your ears. Chain saws, church bells, cars on a highway, trains, the clang of industry, farm animals, the roar of rapids, and the crash of surf are all capable in the right circumstances of giving clues to your position. To judge more accurately from which direction a sound is coming, use only one ear, or cup your hands around both while slowly turning. You'll be able to come within 10 degrees, which is pretty good.

Use your nose. Sailors often speak of smelling land before they see it. Water has smells too. The moisture from any body of water, be it river or ocean, produces a distinctive aroma. Odors from newly mowed lawns, farms, freshly turned earth, wildflowers, factories, oil refineries, and car exhausts can drift long distances downwind, and they're often strongest in fog, mist, or rain.

Don't try to remember every little peculiarity—your memory can't store or use that much information. Don't bother with anything other than the most obvious features beyond your immediate route. Save your concentration for the finer details along your current path. As you proceed, turn around at every junction and landmark. Study what you see. This is the view you'll encounter on your return trip. Think in reverse to maintain the Ariadne Thread that will take you back.

It's always safest to stay on marked roads or trails, not leaving them unless you are positive that you know where you are and how to reach your destination. Trails may seem boring, but they offer the best chance of taking you where you want to go and back. (In many wilderness areas, we are requested to stay on marked trails for another reason, too: to minimize disturbance to surrounding areas, which may include nesting sites, thin soil vulnerable to erosion, and scarce habitat.)

Stay with a trail until it either disappears or heads persistently in the wrong direction. Then head back, or start some serious navigating. Beware of old or marginal-looking trails, which have a way of petering out at inconvenient times. Game trails often lead to nothing more than good forage. Even on a trail, it is good wayfinding procedure to stay in touch with where you are, to take note of landmarks you pass, to relate your position to references, and to remember distances and directions traveled. Trail intersections that look well marked and obvious may look different when approached from the opposite direction. Maintain a running record in your mind of the path you have followed. If the route has been indirect, you might even keep written notes or make simple sketch maps (we'll see how later on); this provides both your current position and the way to get back.

All of this envisioning process and a mosaic of observations are stored in your gray matter as what we have been calling a "mental map." This map is nothing more than an outline of shapes, directions of paths and roads, prominent landmarks, and relative positions of everything in it. Everyone has a substantial catalog of them, one for each place we've been and many for places about which we only dream. Some are too old to read, others are fresh and accurate, and all are unlike anyone else's—because we each see the world differently.

It's important to cultivate the ability to create mental maps, but we can guarantee that what's in your head isn't exactly a Rand McNally atlas. Because we each see the world from a unique perspective, our mental maps are not as accurate as we might like to think (we'll find out why in the next section). Still, practice "drawing" and reading them—they're a great help.

The common link between the loose bits of information in this section is staying aware of your surroundings and maintaining a reference to a constant. With these two principles in mind, you shouldn't get lost. But don't just take this information and store it away; use it in your daily life as you drive to work, pass through a city, enter a new airport terminal, or walk in the park. Practice is important, for navigation in the wilderness or anywhere else is not a technique—it is a habit, a manner of thinking, and an awareness of the land. It is seeing indicators and noticing what is going on around you.

WHY WE GET LOST

Under the definition of *lost*, we come across such dismal synonyms as *helpless*, *desperate*, *denied*, and even *insensible*. You may be one of the few people on the planet who has never felt this aimless despair, but for the rest of us, these words hit home. The question, then, is: If getting lost is so awful, why do we let it happen to us? In part, the answer is that we can't help ourselves.

We seem to have an almost natural ability to do it, which probably makes getting lost our real sixth sense. For a start, we can't even walk in a straight line. Try it. Go to a beach, a field of snow, or any open area where you will leave footprints. Make sure there is no wind or bright sun to act as a reference point. Now, blindfold yourself and try to walk a straight line. You'll probably find that after ⅛ mile, your track has begun to veer. At a ½ mile,

> When I had gone quite a distance over the rocks—far enough, I thought, to be down on the plateau—I stopped and looked around. I couldn't see anything that looked like a trail. I couldn't find a single spot of white paint. I thought I must be down on the plateau, but could not be sure. . . . Boy, it's no fun getting off the trail, when the cloud is so thick you can't see a dozen yards ahead!
>
> —Donn Fendler,
> *Lost on a Mountain in Maine*

there is a noticeable curve and, after a few miles, you might cross your own tracks—making a complete circle. If you walked faster, the circle would tighten.

Actually, it would be remarkable if we didn't walk in circles. It's in our bones—literally. Each of us is built slightly lopsided and asymmetrical. Without visual clues to guide us in a straight line, these imbalances take over and we head off in circles. The most common cause, with the greatest effect, is that one leg is shorter than the other. There seems to be no dominant side; you are as likely to deviate to the left as to the right. And, for no apparent reason, men tend to stray about half as much as women.

Of course, there are those who can't, or won't, accept the obvious. One scientist theorized that there was a natural spiraling influence in the brain of all living creatures. Maybe, but it is the more mundane reasons, such as legs of slightly different length, that actually throw us off course.

Another factor, though less detrimental, is that we usually favor one eye. Instead of looking at a distant object equally through both eyes, we depend on one more than the other. This makes it harder to walk a straight path.

We also angle away from things that bother us. We take the course of least resistance without being aware of it. Wind, rain, and snow from one side make us tend toward the other. We also naturally veer downhill, never uphill. When we come across a minor obstruction, we usually step around it toward our favored side. And, when given a choice, 98 percent of us turn right. Do this enough times and you have begun to go seriously off course.

We rarely have to travel in an absolutely straight line, of course, so this inability is not critical. Admittedly, you might try to cross an open expanse toward a distant landmark, lose it in the haze, and become disoriented. However, that is the exception and there are ways of making sure it doesn't happen, as you'll learn later.

Don't be tempted to wander off into the unknown, depending on a vague assurance that "this feels like the right way." Depend on reliable facts—and beware of unreliable facts. Where do unreliable facts come from? Unfortunately, one of the main sources is your head.

In the previous section, we spoke of mental maps, that is, data banks of stored information about how different parts of our world are pieced together. Everyone has them, and some are better than others. The problem with these maps is that they are based not only on your direct experiences, but also on your indirect experiences. This means that a lot of what is stored up there has been passed on from secondhand sources.

Books, television, photographs, real maps, and conversations (i.e., descriptions of other people's mental maps) all help to sketch out the maps in your mind. It's inevitable. You can't be everywhere, so you must sometimes depend on outside sources. This is not necessarily bad; however, problems arise when our maps are influenced by our prejudices, imagination, and unique perceptions.

For instance, you might read a guidebook that comments on landmarks on a trail or on sights along the way. From the written words, you build an image of what you expect to see; however, it's not always what you find. If you force yourself to be objective, though, you probably have to agree that what was written was an accurate description, and that it was you who read something else into it. This is perfectly normal. We concoct images not so much from the way things are, but rather from the way we think they are, or should be. The two are often very different. Be prepared to revise your preconceptions when they no longer fit your surroundings.

Even when we look at something directly, we constantly modify the information and redraw our mental maps to fit our interpretations. Psychologists say that much of what we imagine to be true about our surroundings is actually unsupported or inferred information. Our mental maps, therefore, are part fact and part fiction. They comprise haphazardly gathered material from direct and indirect sources, often altered to fit our preconceived notions.

To see what I mean, try this: Draw a map of a familiar area and then compare it to a professionally drawn map. You'll begin to get an idea of how biased your vision of the world is. You'll draw what you know best with great accuracy, leave out what is unimportant to you, and often alter size and distance to express your priorities.

This doesn't mean you should ignore the maps in your mind—far from it. They're a vital part of developing a sense of direction, and you need them for a bird's-eye view of where you are. Just don't let them run riot—keep them under control

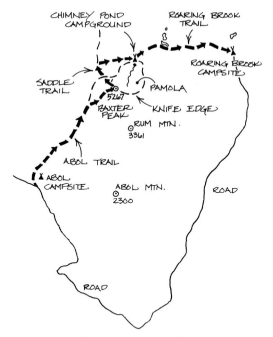

And as traced from a topographic map.

As sketched from the memory of a 12-year-old.

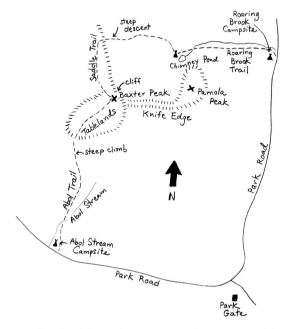

As sketched from the memory of a 42-year-old.

The trail from Abol Stream campground (Baxter State Park, Maine) to Baxter Peak on Mt. Katahdin, then to Chimney Pond campground, then to Roaring Brook campground.

Because our mental maps are imperfect, we must be willing to adjust them when necessary. Note that the older hiker (who was reading a map during the hike) has his directions approximately correct, but his distances are suspect.

from the start. Learn to edit them. Fine-tune your mental maps with information from real (i.e., cartographic) maps, a compass, landmarks, and reference points and lines. One of the easiest ways to get lost is to put too much trust in your unedited mental map and to let your "feelings" overcome your informed good judgment.

The manner in which we "read" cartographic maps is also colored by desire or preconception. We may well envision a landscape that doesn't exist or convince ourselves that a tempting trail isn't going to be too steep to follow. It is the same with photographs of an area that we want to explore, or a description of a goal or landmark—all can be transformed by our preconceived notions of what things should look like. We've all seen the standard photograph of the Matterhorn—that is our image of it. But if we came upon it from a different angle, would the image and the reality mesh?

Information is even more likely to become confused when transferred by the spoken word, as when getting directions. Very often we hear something very different from what was said—it happens all the time. Of course, it is just as likely that those giving the directions don't know what they're talking about in the first place.

Be particularly cautious when asking locals for directions. People who live where you are traveling are often not interested in the same things you are. While they can tell you how to get to a market or the post office, they may not know where a scenic waterfall is. They may have heard of it or visited it once long ago, but it is not part of their daily experience. This is true of all peoples, primitive and civilized. Most Parisians can't offer you more than the vaguest instructions on how to get to the Louvre, but they can give precise directions to a local bank or wine shop.

Then there is pride, which often prevents people from admitting they don't know the way. When you ask for directions, they improvise; sometimes they tell you it's impossible to get there from here.

Asking for directions and picking up local knowledge is half the fun of getting lost. You get colorful advice and meet lots of new folks (whom you will never be able to find again, of course). Don't be too anxious to believe what others tell you. Integrate local knowledge with what you know for sure from your map or compass. And be wary of asking strangers to pinpoint a place on your map. Many are not familiar with maps—they'll jab a finger down anywhere, just to save face and get rid of you.

It's human nature not to admit that you don't know where something is. It's just as difficult to admit that you're lost. The cover-up urge is stronger in some of us than others. Yet, it is important to recognize this shortcoming and acknowledge it when you feel the slight twinge of being disoriented. Don't wait for the twinge to develop into the full-blown panic of being lost. Ignoring the reality that you may be lost is a good way to get thoroughly lost.

We often have no control over the causes of our getting lost, the causes we've just been discussing. They are (to varying degrees) a part of us, so there is an excuse for it. But there is no excuse for getting lost when it can be prevented—that is, when it is only our failure to use good navigational techniques that gets us into trouble.

This usually happens when we forget to keep track of our position. You say to yourself, "I'm only going a short distance. Why bother?" It can occur when you're taking a shortcut off the trail or going for a brief stroll away from camp. Then there are those who see no reason to bother with all that navigating stuff because they are always going to stick to the trails. The fault with that reasoning is that trails have a way of disappearing or being hard to find in the first place. Things are rarely as easy as they look.

Many trails start at the junction of back roads, which themselves are hard to follow and often lead into complex mazes. Then, too, trails cross each other, markers or blazes may be missing or destroyed, or deer or other large animals may have made their own paths that look inviting.

The clearly marked trail on your park map, which looks so obvious and easy to follow, in reality may be old, overgrown, or not much of a trail in the first place. Even on a well-marked trail you can get lost by not watching where you are going. If the going is rough, we tend to watch the ground directly ahead of us, which makes it easy to miss a turn or go off on an unmarked path. Or you may encounter a well-blazed or well-cairned trail made by someone else when they were lost. It happens—in fact, it's common. Then, too, if you don't keep track of where you are, you can lose your feeling for direction when visibility is suddenly limited. Fog, rain, darkness, and snow can make a trail disappear very quickly. Then what?

Off the trail, beaten path, or streets of a familiar city, we lose our way by not clinging to the basic tenets of staying found. You must immediately establish—and then maintain—a reference, keep track of directions and distances traveled, remember landmarks, or aim for a broad target. If you don't, you're a prime candidate for not getting home in time for supper.

We get lost not because of what we do but because of what we don't do. You stay oriented primarily by keeping track of where you are. This is not complicated to do, only taking a little time and effort. Every 15 minutes, or whenever you change direction, estimate where you are. If you're the methodical type, keep track of your position with notes (e.g., "turned west at crossed dead trees, walked 12 minutes to abandoned tractor"). And if you plan to return along the same route, turn around frequently to see what your path will look like on the way back. Watch where you are going.

HOW TO "GET FOUND"

Well, now you've done it. You've been daydreaming, seeing the sights. You've turned a corner and realized you haven't a clue about where you are. Fifteen minutes ago you felt yourself hesitate at a junction; 10 minutes later you didn't recognize an obvious landmark. You were merely disoriented then, but now you're lost. You can't figure out how to retrace your steps; everything looks the same, nothing seems familiar. OK, now what are you going to do?

The first thing is to stop. Don't keep on walking and making the situation worse. Admit that you are lost and that it's probably only going to be a small inconvenience, not a life-threatening episode. Calm yourself. Sit down, have a bite to eat, clear your head, and begin looking for clues. Try to remember where you have been during the last half-hour. Envision the last point where you were sure of your position.

Look around for features that might provide a reference. If nothing registers, but you think that you are not far from somewhere familiar, start navigating from scratch. Identify a landmark, or make

The thought that he was lost fell upon Bullock with the suddenness of a marauder. One moment he was jogging along with eyes on the swaying sled, the next he was scanning the horizon in search of something familiar. His back was torturing him, but he dared not stop. The fact that his dogs might lead him to safety found no place in his consciousness.

—Malcolm Waldron,
Snow Man

one, for your current position so you can find it again. Head out from there to explore a little at a time, returning if you are unsuccessful. (For more detailed information, look ahead to When You Are Lost in chapter 5.)

Since the beginning of long-distance flying, aviators have filed flight plans at their points of departure. These forms list the names of those traveling, their destination, their intended route, gear carried, time of departure, and estimated time of arrival. When they don't show up, the folks back home at least have an idea about which cornfield the wreckage might be in. The system has helped rescuers find many a downed aircraft, and there is no reason not to use the same approach when hiking in a national park or the great unknown. And if you do file a travel plan, remember to tell the folks when you're back. (Caution: Don't leave a travel plan under the windshield wiper of your car at the trailhead. It's an invitation to thieves—there might be no car when you come back.)

When it's obvious that you are lost, try what you can to reorient yourself. If it's hopeless, don't try heading off on a hunch. This is the worst time to start trusting your sixth sense; it's probably what got you lost in the first place. Either use proven navigational techniques to find something you recognize or start making it easy for others to find you.

And next time, do yourself a favor. Watch where you are going and where you have been.

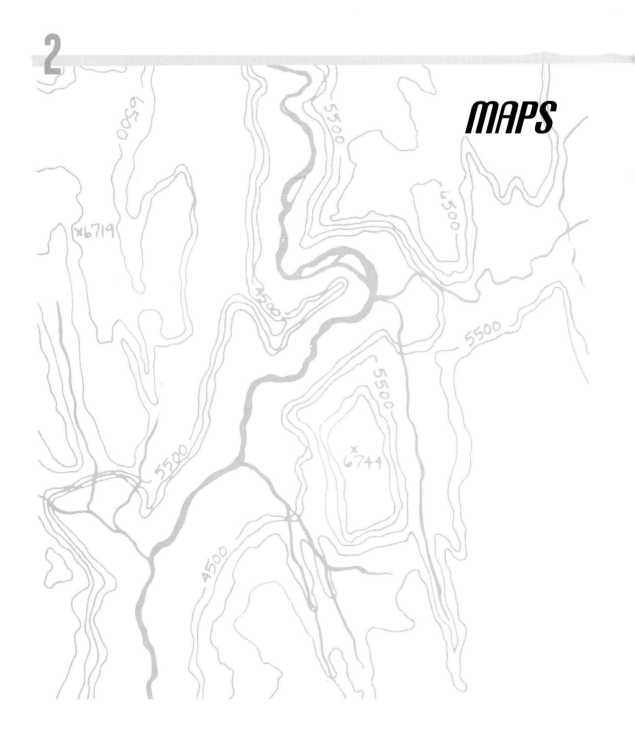

MAPS

After learning to understand road signs, the first navigational tool we are introduced to is the map. We all grow up with them, which is what makes it so strange that there are so many "cartophobes" among us. In this chapter, we'll learn what maps can do and, maybe more important, what they can't. We'll see what truths they hold and how they lie. First, though, you need to learn the language and vocabulary of map symbols. Like books, maps are meant to be read, but a map gives you all its information at once instead of doling it out a page at a time. The trick is to learn how to absorb it in small doses.

Another disorienting attribute of maps is that they convert the full-size, three-dimensional world into a greatly reduced flat one that you can hold in your hands. It is up to the map-reader to reexpand and inflate that tiny, flat landscape in his mind's eye. The conceptual gymnastics required for this take practice—more so because maps are drawn as if for birds looking down at the world rather than for earth-bound creatures like us.

So we'll find out how to identify from the side all the features that maps depict from above. And, finally, we'll explore the arcane art of map-folding.

A word of warning, however: this chapter will be wasted if you don't get out there with map in hand, wander around, get lost, get found, and see what maps are all about. Read and practice; by the end of this chapter, you'll be a master.

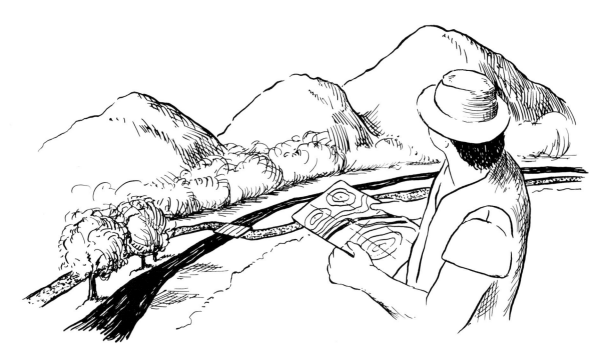

Map properly folded and oriented with the landscape.

THE WORLD IN YOUR HANDS

Once you understand their language, maps speak volumes. They show what can't be seen, identify what you can see, help plan your route and choose a campsite, warn of potential hazards, lead you to areas of beauty, and—by providing directions and distances to known landmarks—pinpoint your position.

The modern cartographer's art creates an accurate and comprehensive document that, with practice, is easier to read than the explanations that follow. Good maps are the quintessential explainers, part of our way of thinking. We "map out" plans of attack; we ask plaintively if we have to "draw a map" when describing something obvious.

Many of us have never learned to read maps because there seemed to be no need. We blindly follow the road signs or the blazes on a trail. But if we miss a sign or stray from the path, we're in trouble. Wayfinding then becomes like playing an instrument without being able to read music. You can do it, but you'll always be handicapped.

Unfortunately, no map can be taken at pure face value. Maps have been called "truth compressed into symbols," and they need to be interpreted. They're not exact replicas and, therefore, require imagination to get out what has been put in. The navigator's job, as interpreter, is to compare the map with the real world, which is more than a simple exercise in spatial relationships. Envisioning the full-size, three-dimensional world greatly reduced and flat takes special ability, which comes only from practice.

Although maps offer a lot, no map can tell you everything. The best navigators are those who augment map data with as much outside information and experience as possible. They also plan ahead for alternative routes and landmarks in case what a map shows doesn't seem to be there. Don't take any map literally, particularly with regard to road and trail systems, which tend to change between map editions. Look for significant features within the general pattern of details. To get the most from maps, you must know when to go beyond them.

In Maps We Trust... Sometimes

There is a big difference between having a map with you and being able to read that map. Take, for instance, a couple of hikers I met while working as a wilderness ranger in Grand Gulch, Utah. I was camped near the mouth of a nice side canyon. The dinner I was cooking was nearly done. I heard them before I saw them come through the sagebrush. They were gnarly-looking, tired, and dust-covered, and I figured they were going to camp nearby because the only water for miles around was right here.

They stopped abruptly and seemed startled to see me. "This one doesn't have water flowing out of it either!" one of them exclaimed. "There's water nearby," I said as I introduced myself as the ranger. "No, no," the other said, "we're going to camp at the junction of Grand Gulch and Bullet Canyon. It's part of our loop."

"Well"," I said, "if that junction was your destination today, you missed your mark by about 8 miles."

"What!" the second hiker exclaimed.

"Sure," I said, "Ya'll boys walked right past the junction quite a while ago. Here's where you are now." I pointed to the map in the hands of a bewildered, slack-jawed navigator.

His hiking partner had had enough, apparently. He let the obscenities fly as he dropped his pack and brought up his fists. "I told you that was it, but you had to keep going," he shouted.

"Hold on," I said, intervening in what was sure to be a knock-down-drag-out. "What was it that made you think that it wasn't Bullet Canyon?"

"Because the map showed flowing water there," the navigator replied.

"Well, that was definitely your first mistake. You see, this is the desert and nothing really flows year-round, even if the map shows it that way. Next time," I said, "instead of trusting whether there is flowing water or not, count the side canyons that come into the main canyon. That way, you know where you're at and there's no supposition."

PJC

TYPES OF MAPS

Maps are scaled-down representations of the earth's surface, and different types of maps do this in different ways. The style with which you are probably most familiar is the *planimetric* map, which gets its name from the Latin words *planus* (even or flat) and *metrum* (measure). It represents the world as if it were all a level surface—without mountains or valleys, mesas or canyons—so there's a lot that planimetric maps aren't telling you. What they lose in natural features, they make up for with information about man-made features.

For outdoor wayfinding, the least useful planimetric map is the grade-school version, showing only towns and political boundaries—the kind by which Huck Finn was navigating. A planimetric road map for automobiles is slightly more useful; more useful still are the visitors' guides provided at parks and those available from the U.S. Forest Service and the National Park Service (see the appendix). These maps show trails, roads, streams, rivers, rangers' stations, and campgrounds in great detail. They are more than sufficient for finding your way in well-marked parks when you're sure that you won't be leaving the trails.

The most useful maps for our purposes are *topographic* (top-oh-GRAPH-ic) maps. These describe the *terrain*—the shape of the landscape, its ups and downs—as well as some man-made features. They are ideal for hikers, campers, hunters, fishermen, cross-country skiers, and anyone else who may forsake the beaten path. They are of value even if you stick to the trails; by painting a more accurate perception of the landscape, they offer you a better chance to keep track of your position. Planimetrics often show trails and roads that are not on topographics, and topographics show natural features you won't find on planimetrics. If you can, carry both types or transfer information to your topographic map before departing.

There are topos (TOE-poes), as they are casually referred to, covering almost every square inch of the United States, its territories and protectorates, Canada, and a good part of the remaining world. In the United States, they are compiled by the U.S. Geological Survey (USGS), which now has a library of about 54,000. You can purchase topos directly from the USGS by mail or phone, or from local outdoor shops (see the appendix for map sources).

To make ordering easy, each state has been subdivided into *quadrangles*—commonly known as *quads*—based on lines of longitude and latitude. Simply choose the quad you want from a free state index. Quads are named for towns or prominent geographical features. USGS maps are made to extremely high standards: at least 90 percent of all points surveyed must be accurate to within $\frac{1}{50}$ of an inch on the map. You won't miss much with a USGS topo for your guide. Costing only a few dollars, these maps are true bargains.

If you're traveling by water, maps are properly called *charts*. Nautical charts carry very little information about the land (usually only along the shore) but a lot about the water and what is under it. They show depths, bottom features, what the bottom is made of, and the positions of navigational aids such as buoys and lighthouses. The National Ocean Service (NOS) compiles charts for coastal waters and the Great Lakes. The Army Corps of Engineers covers the navigable inland waterways, lakes, and rivers. For camping by canoe or kayak, you can get by with just a topo, but when heading into open or coastal waters, carry a nautical chart too.

There are other more esoteric varieties of maps available—even enhanced aerial photographs—but nothing beats the USGS topos for value, accuracy, and availability. We use them as a standard navigational tool throughout this book.

Because it takes almost five years to generate new USGS topos, they are revised only when absolutely necessary. The last field check on the average topo may have been done about thirty years ago. Forest Service and Park Service maps, as well as some that are privately produced (e.g., the *Trails Illustrated* series), tend to be updated more frequently. Although even the latest map can be dated, it's the man-made features—including bridges, roads, trails, and campgrounds—that are most likely to change. Natural topographical features rarely vary. It is wise to supplement maps with information from the latest guidebooks, park rangers, naturalists, and travelers you trust.

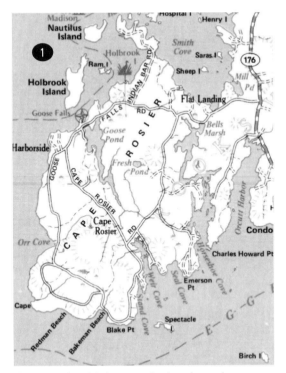

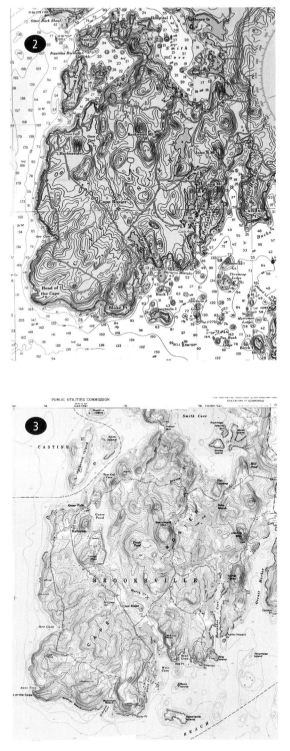

Cape Rosier, Maine, as depicted on three map types. 1. Planimetric road map from DeLorme Mapping Company's Maine Gazetteer. 2. National Ocean Survey chart. 3. USGS topographic map. Each emphasizes different features.

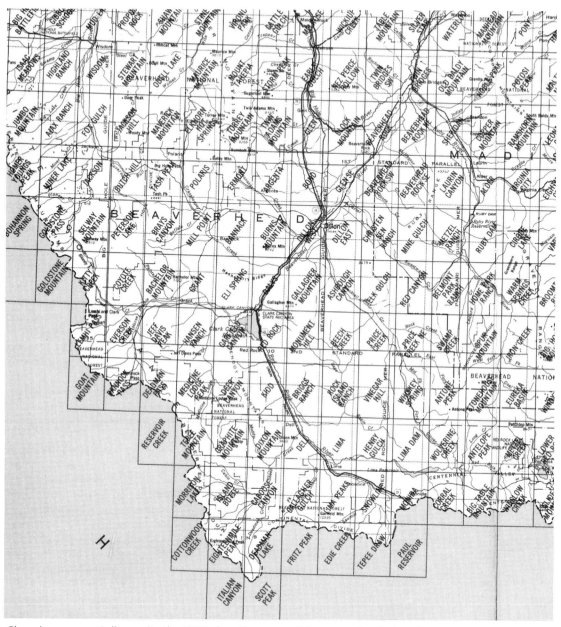

Choosing a map: Call or write the USGS (see the appendix) to get a free Index of Topographical Maps *for the state in which you are traveling. From another map, such as a road map, find the area of interest, noting names of towns or prominent natural features. Locate this area on the index by estimating its position and matching names. Shown here is part of the 7.5-minute topographical map coverage of Montana, taken from the USGS Montana Index. The index also shows the 1:50,000, 1:100,000, and 1:250,000 scale coverages of the state and lists various specialty maps such as standard and shaded relief 1:125,000 topos of Yellowstone National Park.*

THREE DIMENSIONS INTO TWO

Maps take a god's-eye view of the world, looking down and seeing what we cannot. We mortals have limited horizons, seeing only small portions of the world from a decidedly lower point of view.

Relating the compressed, two-dimensional descriptions on a map to the full-size, three-dimensional world can be a daunting task for the imagination. At first, what is represented on the map looks nothing at all like the world around you—that is, until you learn to see.

Start by picking out obvious landmarks and finding your position among them. Next, to get a sense of scale, judge the distances between landmarks and then between them and yourself. Do the same each time you use a map for a new area. It takes time to get the proper perspective, but it must be done or you'll confuse rivers with streams and hills with mountains.

A rugged southwestern landscape as depicted (1) on a topo map (simplified for reproduction purposes), and (2) from a buzzard's-eye view. Your view south from the spot marked "X" would look like illustration (3).

Part 1. Symbols

If we are to interpret a map's message successfully, we must first understand its language—the language of maps is symbols. It's a purely visual and very descriptive means of communication that is done with a surprisingly modest vocabulary of lines, colors, and forms.

Shown on page 33 are the principal symbols, the basic vocabulary of the USGS "dictionary." The best way to make sense of them is to relate each symbol to what it represents. If you don't have a USGS topo map, you can refer to the color maps in this book for the following discussions.

Because cartographers try to make symbols look like what they represent, most are self-explanatory, which is why the symbols used in USGS topos are so similar to those found on maps from private companies, as well as those from other nations. Canadian topos are very handy in that a complete list of symbol descriptions is printed on each map. U.S. maps have only a few listed; you are expected to carry the free pamphlet, *Topographic Map Symbols* (see the appendix). For U.S. nautical charts, a complete book of symbols is in the former NOS publication *Chart No. 1* (see the appendix).

To be legible, symbols are often drawn slightly oversized. The symbol for a school, for example, might be larger than the scale structure. However, the middle of the symbol is always over the location of the building's center. Because of the width of printed lines, roads, trails, streams, and small rivers also may not be to scale, but their centerlines are accurately plotted.

Color is used to enhance information or make it more obvious. The USGS has standardized its use of color as follows:

Black: Man-made features such as roads, trails, railroads, and buildings. Names are always in black.

Blue: Waterways such as lakes, rivers, canals, swamps, and marshes. The contour lines of glaciers and permanent snowfields are also blue.

Brown: Contour lines and elevations.

Green: Substantial vegetation, woods, scrub, orchards, and groves.

White: No vegetation, cleared land, and areas with sparse or scattered foliage.

Red: Larger, more important roads and surveying lines.

Purple: Overprinting. Revisions added from aerial photographs but not yet field-checked.

Some state-produced maps make do with just one color. The USGS does not offer monochromatic maps, whereas Canada has several in both color and monochrome. These maps represent different areas in tones of gray. They are more difficult to interpret, but are cheaper and make better photocopies (for everyone on a trip). Notes in colored ink (i.e., red or blue) also stand out better.

Map-reading is not an instinctive skill; rather, it's an acquired one. It comes from the practice of comparing the world on the map with the one you see around you. To learn a language, you must use it. Pick up a map, go outside, and look around. It will be an enjoyable education.

Part 2. The Legend

The margins of a map contain its legend. Like a fine frame around a painting, the legends around USGS topos improve and enhance the maps. Here's the information they provide. The letters refer to labels on the map on pages 34–35.

A. *Who created the map.* In this case, the U.S. Department of the Interior's Geological Survey and New York State's Department of Transportation.

B. *The title.* The title takes its name from the quadrangle (i.e., Fish's Eddy). All states are subdivided into rectangles (i.e., quadrangles) based on lines of latitude and longitude. They are usually named for a town or prominent natural feature within the quadrangle. The state (New York) and county (Delaware) are also given.

C. *Series.* The USGS categorizes maps by "series" according to how much land is covered. The most common is the 7.5-minute series, which means that each side of the map is 7.5 minutes long, or ⅛ of a degree. As you'll see later, navigators divide the world into degrees. Each degree consists of 60 minutes. A 7.5-minute–series map is 7.5 minutes of latitude high by 7.5 minutes of longitude wide. There is also a 15-minute series covering 15 minutes (¼ of a degree) of latitude and 15 minutes of longitude.

D. *Names of adjoining quadrangles.* These are in parentheses, with one at each corner and one on each side. If the road you are following goes off the map, you know which new quadrangle to order so you can continue your journey. In this example, the left-hand, western border abuts against the Hancock quad.

   Beneath each quad name are numbers and letters in small print; these are *quad codes* used by the U.S. Department of Defense.

E. *Corners.* Each corner is marked with its latitude and longitude. On this 7.5-minute map, the corners are 7.5 minutes apart.

F. *Latitude.* Every 2.5 minutes of latitude is marked by a fine black line along the right (eastern) and left (western) borders. Latitude in the Northern Hemisphere increases as you go north, toward the top of the map. Degrees are usually omitted, with only minutes and seconds shown. There are 60 seconds in a minute.

G. *Longitude.* Every 2.5 minutes of longitude is marked by a fine black line along the top and bottom borders. Longitude in the western hemisphere increases as you go toward the left (west) side of the map. Degrees are usually omitted, with only minutes and seconds shown.

H. *Latitude-longitude intersections.* Lines of latitude and longitude are indicated by crosses where they would intersect.

I. *Plane coordinate system.* There may be other fine black marks on the border with designations such as "690,000 feet." These are part of that state's plane coordinate system.

J. *Grid ticks.* The fine blue lines along the borders are Universal Transverse Mercator (UTM) grid "ticks," part of an international reference system. Each is separated by 1 kilometer (or about ⅝ mile), which makes a handy scale.

K. *Map-creation information.* This block of copy gives information about who did what, how they did it, and what sort of projection (in this example, polyconic) was used to make the map. It also tells when the map was made, which is important. This one was compiled in 1963 and field-checked in 1965.

L. *Revised information* is always in purple. This map was edited in 1982 from aerial photographs taken in 1981. The information has not been field-checked. This gives you a good idea of how up-to-date the map is.

M. *Another title block* with the quad's name, state, key latitude and longitude, and map series. The dates of the last field check and revisions are listed below this information.

N. *Key.* Some maps show a key to road symbols, but rarely anything more.

O. *The quadrangle location* indicates its position within the state.

P. *The scale.* Here, one unit of measurement on the map equals 24,000 units full-size. The USGS uses the 1:24,000 scale for most of its 7.5-minute series: 1 inch equals 2,000 feet—about ⅜ mile. The 15-minute–series maps use a scale of 1:62,500: 1 inch equals 1 mile. The third common scale for U.S. topos is 1:250,000 (1 inch equals 4 miles), which provides the "big picture" needed for expedition planning.

Q. *The bar scales* allow you to make scaled measurements of distance in miles, feet, and kilometers.

R. *Contour interval* is the vertical distance (i.e., the change in elevation) between the brown contour lines. These are lines joining areas of equal height. The National Geodetic Vertical Datum is the reference point for all such elevations.

S. *National Map Accuracy Standards.* Horizontal accuracy: "Not more than 10 percent of the points tested shall be in error by more than ¹⁄₅₀ inch." Vertical accuracy: "Not more than 10 percent of the elevations tested shall be in error by more than half the contour interval."

T. *The declination diagram* shows the direction to the geographic north pole (shown by a star, pointing to the top of the globe), the magnetic north (MN) pole, which is to what a compass points, and the grid north (GN) pole, which we may ignore.

CONTROL DATA AND MONUMENTS

Horizontal control:

With third order or better elevation .... BM △ 148

Checked spot elevation .... △ 64

Vertical control:

Third order or better, with tablet .... BM × 53

Third order or better, recoverable mark .... × 394

BOUNDARIES

State or territorial ....

County or equivalent ....

Civil township or equivalent ....

Park, reservation, or monument ....

LAND SURVEY SYSTEMS

Land grant or mining claim; monument .... ·· — ⊡

ROADS AND RELATED FEATURES

Primary highway ....

Secondary highway ....

Light duty road ....

Unimproved road .... = = = = =

Trail ....

Bridge ....

Drawbridge ....

BUILDINGS AND RELATED FEATURES

Dwelling or place of employment: small; large . ▪ ▨

School; church .... ♪ ⚲

Airport ....

Well (other than water); windmill .... ○ ⚥

Water tank: small; large... ● ⊘

Gaging station .... ◉

Landmark object .... ⊙

Campground; picnic area .... ⚘ ⛱

Cemetery: small; large.. ⌋†⌊ Cem

RAILROADS AND RELATED FEATURES

Standard gauge single track; station .... ┼──•──

CONTOURS

Topographic:

Intermediate ....

Index ....

Depression ....

MINES AND CAVES

Quarry or open pit mine.. ⚔

Gravel, sand, clay, or borrow pit .... ⚒

Mine tunnel or cave entrance............................... ⊰

SURFACE FEATURES

Sand or mud area, dunes, or shifting sand....

Intricate surface area...

Gravel beach or glacial moraine ....

VEGETATION

Woods ....

Scrub..

Orchard ....

COASTAL FEATURES

Rock bare or awash.. ✳

Exposed wreck ....

Depth curve; sounding... 10

Breakwater, pier, jetty, or wharf...........................

Seawall ....

RIVERS, LAKES, AND CANALS

Intermittent stream ....

Perennial stream...

Perennial river...

Large falls; large rapids..

Masonry dam ....

SUBMERGED AREAS AND BOGS

Marsh or swamp..

The more frequently encountered symbols on standard-edition U.S. topos. With few exceptions, the Canadian symbols are the same.

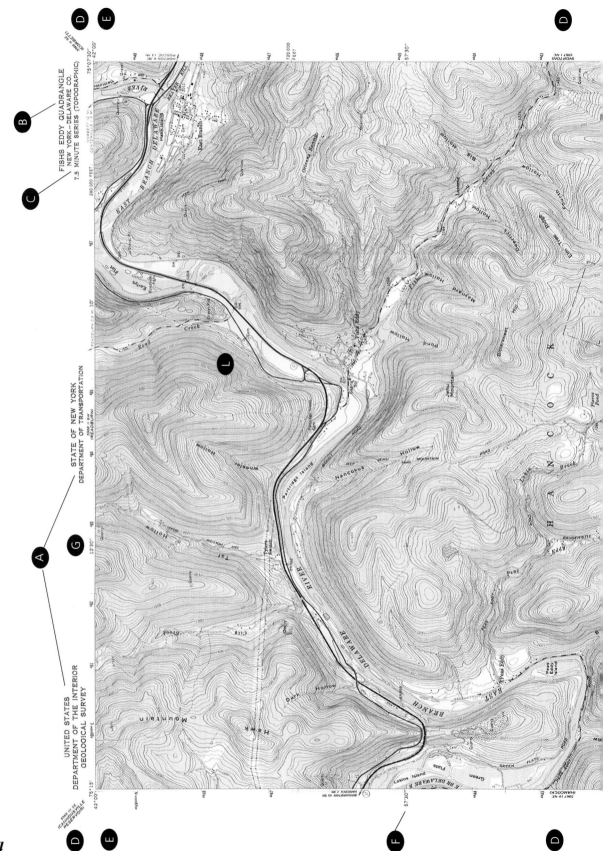

FISHS EDDY QUADRANGLE
NEW YORK–DELAWARE CO.
7.5 MINUTE SERIES (TOPOGRAPHIC)

STATE OF NEW YORK
DEPARTMENT OF TRANSPORTATION

UNITED STATES
DEPARTMENT OF THE INTERIOR
GEOLOGICAL SURVEY

34

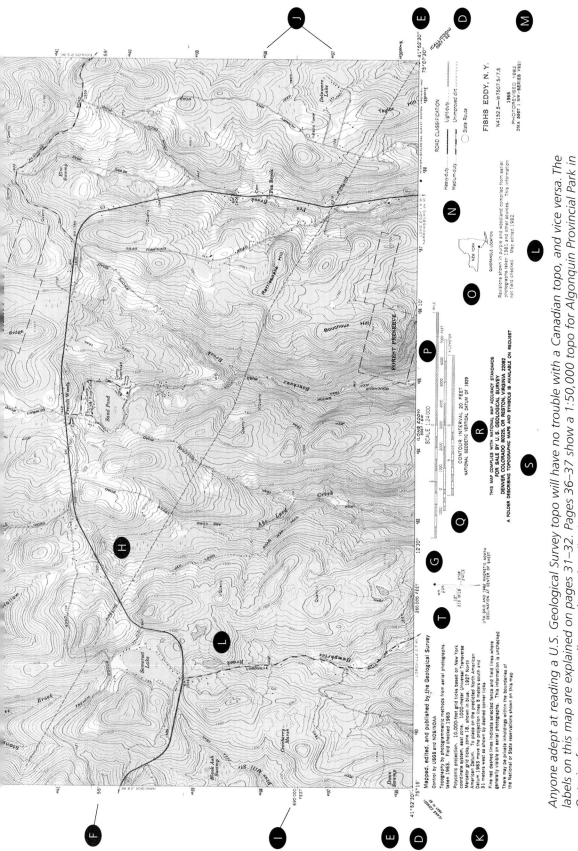

Anyone adept at reading a U.S. Geological Survey topo will have no trouble with a Canadian topo, and vice versa. The labels on this map are explained on pages 31–32. Pages 36–37 show a 1:50,000 topo for Algonquin Provincial Park in Ontario; features corresponding to those described on pages 31–32 are labeled.

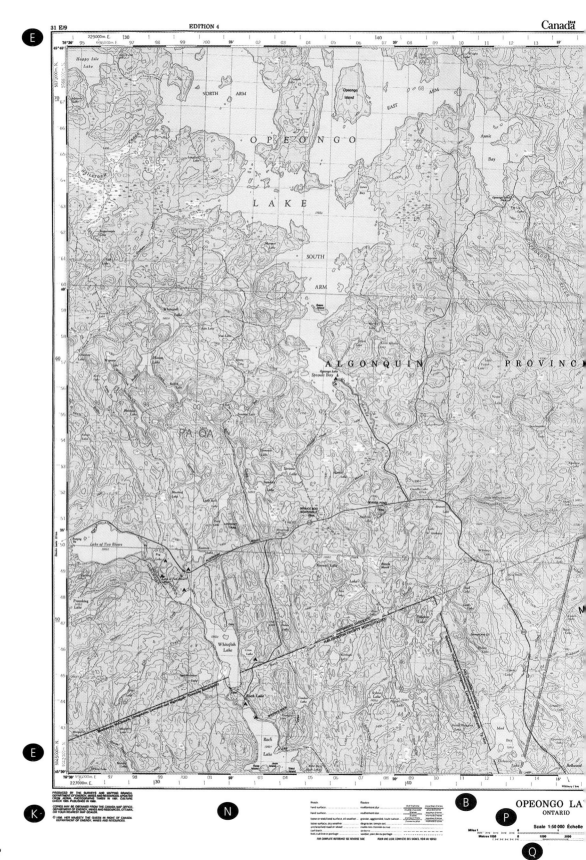

OPEONGO LA
ONTARIO

Scale 1:50 000 Échelle

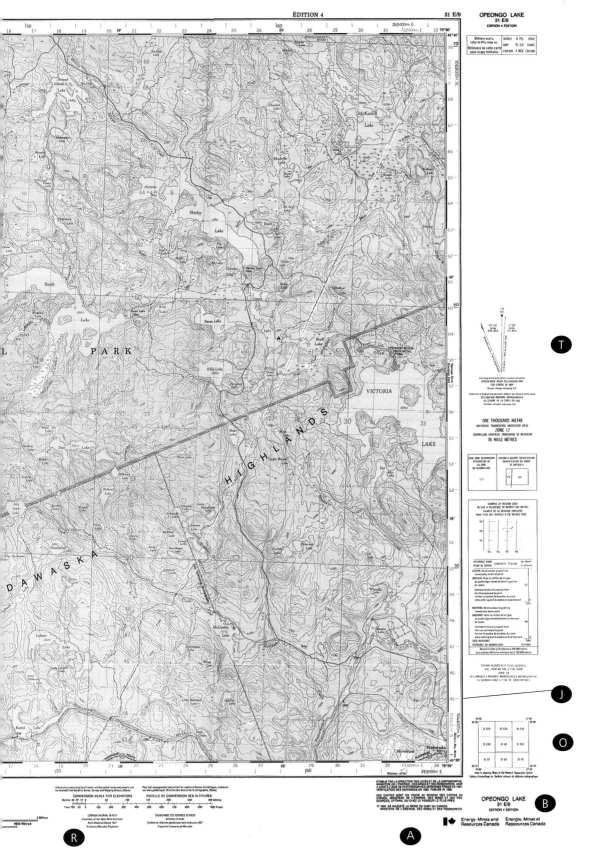

OPEONGO LAKE
31 E/9
EDITION 4 ÉDITION

ONE THOUSAND METRE
UNIVERSAL TRANSVERSE MERCATOR GRID
ZONE 17
QUADRILLAGE UNIVERSEL TRANSVERSE DE MERCATOR
DE MILLE MÈTRES

OPEONGO LAKE
31 E/9
EDITION 4 ÉDITION

Energy, Mines and
Resources Canada

Énergie, Mines et
Ressources Canada

How to Measure It

On almost all maps, when the printing is right side up, geographic north will be at the top. This enables you to find the four cardinal points with great ease. But what about the other 356 degrees? How do you find them?

Here's how. Let's say you have marked your position on a map and want to find the direction to somewhere else, such as the top of a far-off hill. To do this, you need a pencil, a straightedge (e.g., a ruler, an edge of the map flopped over on itself, or a folded piece of paper), and a cheap plastic protractor.

1. Begin by drawing lines of latitude and longitude, using the marks on the borders and crosses on the map. You now have north–south and east–west reference lines to use for this and future problems.
2. From your marked position, draw a straight line (i.e., your course line) through the hill's summit until it intersects a reference line (e.g., a line of latitude, longitude, or any one of the map's borders).
3. Place the base of the protractor (the 0- to 180-degree line) on the reference line and its center over your direction line.
4. Read the number of degrees off the protractor to give you the angle between the reference line and your course line. This may provide your direction right away or you may need to use some simple arithmetic.

2.

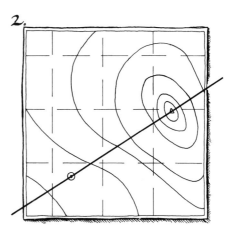

3.

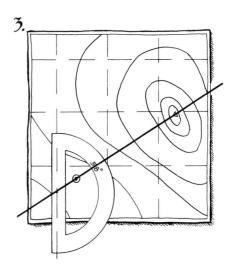

1.

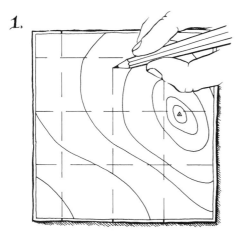

4.

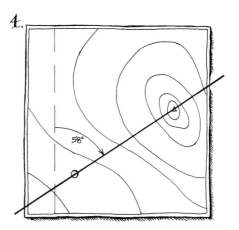

PUTTING YOURSELF ON THE MAP

Finding Your Position

If a map is reduced reality, then by envisioning ourselves brought down to scale (e.g., at 1:24,000, you'd be about 0.003 inch tall), we can walk through both worlds—the real one and the map's—at the same time. As we pick out a landmark in one, we can relate it to the other, thus keeping track of our ever-changing position.

To do this, start by identifying your initial location on the map, a single spot. Once this is done,

you then have to orient (i.e., align) the map to the surrounding world to maintain the illusion of map and reality being as one. First, let's find out where you are, then follow with how to orient the map. To locate your starting position, and any spot thereafter, you can use one of the following two methods on the map:

1. *Landmarks.* If you are standing at an obvious and well-defined location, you know where you are on the map. This could be a building, the foot of a bridge, a bench mark at a summit, a fire tower, a sign, the spot where a road ends,

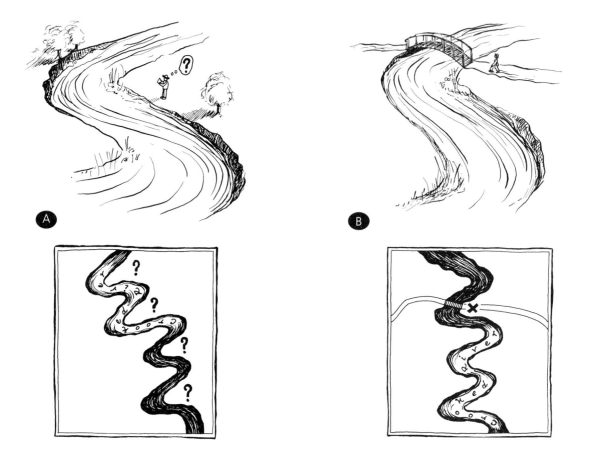

The A drawings illustrate what can happen when you use only one reference line. by using crossed reference lines (see text page 55), illustrated in the B drawings above, you can pinpoint your position within a much narrower range.

a waterfall, or anything else that is unique and can be matched to a symbol on the map.

2. *Crossed reference lines.* A reference line is an easily identifiable elongated feature. If you're standing near a road, trail, river, tree line, railroad track, shoreline, overhead power line, backbone of a ridge, or the base of a narrow valley, you're next to a reference line. A good reference line is recognizable enough to stand out from the surrounding landscape and is clearly indicated on the map.

Once you have found your reference line on the map, you can say with assurance that you are somewhere on it—you just don't know where. This may not sound like a good way of finding out where you are, but it does eliminate everything else in the world except that one line—which is quite a lot of real estate.

To make that reference line into a single identifiable spot, you must cross it with another reference line. Let's say you're on Mediterranean Avenue; that's your reference line. But where on Mediterranean? After a short walk, you come to an intersection. It's Boardwalk, another reference line. Where the two cross each other makes a point, or a *fix* (because it fixes your position). Your position is now pinpointed, and that is the only place where you could be.

Other fixes could be from where a trail fords a river, a railroad crossing, a ridge ending in a cliff, a fork in a road, or where a road meets a lake's shore. If you look carefully, there are crossed reference lines everywhere. You can also create a reference line from a transit or range. When two objects appear to overlap with one behind the other, putting themselves into alignment from your point of view, they form a range. If you draw a line on the map connecting the two objects, you are somewhere on it.

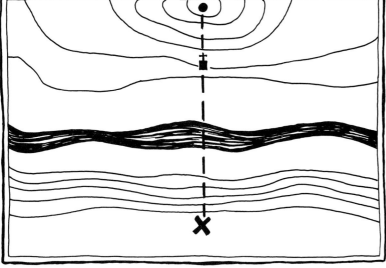

Reference line from a transit or range.

Orienting the Map

To successfully use a map as a direction-finding tool, you have to correlate it to the world it represents. Luckily, it is easy to orient a map—all you have to do is look around and align the map with the surrounding landscape. Once this relationship is established, you can plan routes and explore with confidence. Begin by looking for easily identifiable features such as peaks, clearings, buildings, and roads that are also on the map. Compare what you see to what is on the map, turning the map until it relates to what you see. If something is ahead of you, it should be ahead of your position on the map; if something is to your right, it should be to the right of your position on the map. Once this is accomplished, you're oriented. By keeping the map oriented as you travel, with the direction of travel forward, it is easier to relate what you see to what is on the map, reducing the risk of getting lost. Orienting the map also gives you an approximate idea of your location, although not as accurately as with a landmark or crossed lines of reference.

The only problem with keeping a map oriented is that you might wind up holding it at an angle or even upside down, making it difficult to read names, notes, and symbols. Some folks hold their maps right side up (i.e., north on top) regardless of the direction they are facing; however, this can cause considerable visual juggling because when heading south; for example, anything to your left on the map is actually to your right. Interpreting the world in reverse can be very disorienting, but some people can and prefer to do it. In general, orienting the map is the better and more reliable method, allowing you to determine directions directly.

There may be times when it is impossible to orient a map by observation alone, such as when you're in a deep wood, on a barren plain, or in any landscape devoid of mapped features. Sometimes too many features can be just as bad. If you are surrounded by endless hills, it might be impossible to tell one from another. In any of these cases, the only way to orient the map and yourself is with a compass, which we discuss in chapter 3.

Orienting Yourself

Once you've got the map oriented so that it matches the land, you can . . .

Identify Unknown Landmarks

With the map oriented, put one end of a straight-edge, such as a pencil or stick, on your known position. Turn the straightedge until it points to the landmark in the field that you want to identify. Now study the map where the straightedge lies; the unknown landmark will be on that line. Find it by matching features such as elevation, foliage, shapes, and distance from your position.

Find Your Approximate Location

If you are not near any mapped landmarks or crossed lines of reference, you can get a rough approximation of your position by *triangulation*. With the map oriented, find at least two (three are better) distant landmarks that are also on the map. Put the center of a straightedge, such as a pencil or stick, across the spot marking one of the landmarks. Rotate the straightedge until one end points to the actual landmark. When this is done, the opposite end points toward your position. Draw a long line in that direction, then do the same with the other landmarks; where the lines meet is your approximate position.

It will be best to do this with the map on the ground rather than in your hands. Don't be fooled by lines meeting at one nice, neat point. This technique is only a rough (although very useful) way of finding an approximate position (we'll do it by compass with considerably more accuracy later). Check the landscape around you to see if the point where the lines meet makes sense.

MAP CARE AND GEAR

Good topo maps are relatively inexpensive, so it's easy to think of them as expendable—and they are, if you're near a store where they can be replaced. However, in the wilds, this won't be possible: take care of your maps.

Folding

One of the best ways to extend a map's life is to fold it. A properly folded map stays out of harm's way in pocket or pack, is simple to refold without resorting to origami, and is convenient to use in high winds. The method shown opposite is an adaptation of the classic commuter's newspaper-fold. It makes a compact package that lets you look at any part of the map without having to open it all the way. Fold lines are parallel to the borders, making it easy to find the cardinal directions.

Protection

If you're going to be out in foul weather or in a boat, you might want to apply a water-repellent coating to your maps. That's "water repellent," not "waterproof"—which can only be done by lamination and is expensive and makes the map almost impossible to fold.

A water-resistant coating can be applied with spray-on lacquers or acrylics found at art-supply stores. Spray both sides in a series of light coats rather than one heavy coat, which may give you blobs of glop that change the topography. Specialty map stores carry sprays or liquids specifically made for the job, usually costing more than the map they are designed to protect. These shops may also carry map pouches in leather, canvas, or plastic. Keeping your map in a protective cover prevents the folds from wearing and corners from curling over; however, most store-bought covers are unnecessarily bulky. By far, the best (and cheapest) protection is a resealable plastic bag; when it gets too beat up, you can use it to hold your lunch.

Paraphernalia

- Keep your chosen route from getting lost in a tangle of contour lines by using a yellow high-lighter to make the route stand out at a glance. Bring along a pencil stub with its eraser still intact and a knife (always a good idea anyway) to give it a fine point.
- A pocket magnifying glass helps clarify information printed in tiny "mouse type" and count densely crowded contour lines.

The Lie of the Land

Do maps lie? Not really—but sometimes they don't tell the whole truth. Remember Huck Finn and Tom Sawyer's balloon flight? Huck knew they were still over Illinois because the land below was green, not pink—which any fool knew was the color of Indiana.

When Tom asked what color had to do with it, Huck replied, "It's got everything to do with it. Illinois is green and Indiana is pink . . . I've seen it on the map, and it's pink."

When Tom questioned this interpretation, Huck said, "Well, what's a map for? Ain't it to learn you facts?"

"Of course."

"Well, then, how's it going to do that if it lies?"

In his own way, Huck was right. While some maps come close, none is perfectly accurate. They can't show every barn, chicken coop, and rock outcrop, nor can they precisely indicate what a swamp, meadow, or woods is like or how the land changes. Impassable cliffs, for example, may lurk unmarked between contour lines.

New roads are always being built and old trails overgrown. Maps more than a few years old may be substantially out of date. Change is constant. Why, on some newfangled maps, Indiana ain't even pink no more.

- A plastic (because it won't affect a compass) ruler gives you a straightedge for drawing and a way to measure scaled distances. If there's room, carry a 12-inch ruler; if not, a 6-inch one will do.
- The millimeter side of the ruler can be useful even if you're not into metric. Forget that they're millimeters. Just think of those closely spaced, logically numbered, easy-to-count marks as a general measuring tool. Isn't it easier to read the map distance between two points as 38 "somethings" rather than 1¹³⁄₁₆ inches? You can also use the millimeter marks to interpolate between indicated lines of latitude and longitude.
- Finally, you need a cheap, clear-plastic, grade-school protractor to show directions in degrees. If you have the room, a semicircular one with a 6-inch rule on the bottom does double service.
- When choosing navigational equipment, go low-tech, replaceable, affordable, rugged, and reliable.

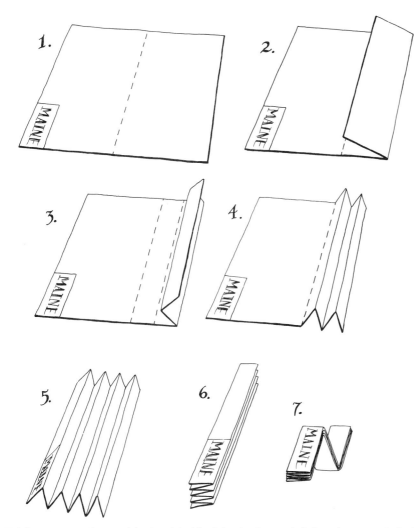

Folding a topo. Start with the title block in the lower left-hand corner. Rub the folds down hard with a fingernail to make sharp creases. Finish with the title block on top.

3

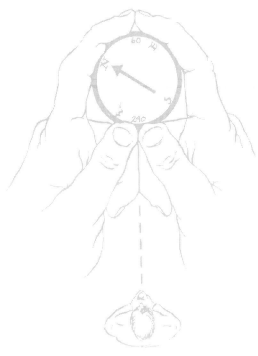

There aren't many things in this world that you can trust implicitly, but a compass is one of them. Few man-made objects are more worthy of your confidence. Of course, the compass does have its idiosyncrasies; however, once understood, it's one of the most reliable pieces of hardware you'll ever acquire. It won't let you down. The golden rule is this: when you're confused and disoriented, trust your compass.

Perversely, this seems just what we are least likely to do when lost, preferring to defer to that creature of fiction—our sense of direction. A not-uncommon phrase heard from those recently rescued is that when they consulted their compass, "There seemed to be something wrong with the damn thing." There hardly ever is.

But it's hard to have confidence in a primitive gadget and the unseen force of magnetism. Although, in principle, you might be willing to suspend your suspicions while reading this in the warm comfort of your living room, would you be able to do so out on the trail, when everything looks like everything else and nothing looks as it should? Well, if you're going to be a successful navigator, you have to make this leap of faith. You must learn to trust your compass and to let go of your preconceptions. Don't be afraid to alter your mental map.

The following pages explain how compasses work, what they are capable of doing, their limitations, and their quirks. Once you've read this, you really should head outdoors and prove to yourself that you can trust your compass. Confidence comes only with practice.

Later in this chapter is a section on the types of compasses. Select one that you think might suit you, then buy an inexpensive model. Experiment until you feel comfortable and secure with this wonderfully simple—yet unfailingly trustworthy—piece of magic.

WHAT COMPASSES CAN DO

Most of us have owned a compass, and many of us have been lost at least once while carrying one. Merely being able to find north won't—by itself—keep you from getting lost. You have to keep track of north (and, therefore, south, east, and west) from the very start of and all through your journey. A compass shows only directions, not position.

As discussed in chapter 1, one of the basic requirements for not getting lost is always to maintain a constant reference point or line to which you can relate. Without that, you have nothing to work from, nothing of substance on which to base your choice of directions. By always pointing north (and south), a compass gives you that reference. If you start with and maintain that reference, here are some of the things a compass can do for you:

- By checking the compass to find your intended direction of travel when first heading out, you'll be able to tell later (when you're not quite sure of things) whether you're coming or going.
- A compass keeps you pointed in the right direction in the absence of a trail or markers.
- If you know your general direction of travel, a compass can help you make the right choice at a fork in the trail.
- People tend to veer to one side as we walk, but a compass keeps us headed in a straight line.

- A compass can help you walk toward something you can't see because it's either too far off or obscured by trees, fog, snow, or darkness.
- When you deviate from your direct course to get around an obstruction, a compass helps (but only helps) get you back on track toward your destination.
- If you walk a direct compass course to somewhere, you can return by following that course in reverse.
- By keeping track of each change of direction and distance traveled, you can return to your starting point even if you followed no fixed outward route.
- A compass gets you back to a line of reference, such as a road or river, after you've been wandering haphazardly.
- You can return to a spot by noting compass directions, or bearings, to landmarks around it. If, when you return, the compass directions to all the landmarks are the same, then you have found that spot.

A compass can do all this and more if you apply some ingenuity—and, when used with a map, it can do even more. A compass makes orienting the map easier and more accurate. In addition, you can pinpoint your position, identify landmarks, and find courses to far-off destinations. Chapter 4 covers the essentials of using a map and compass together. For now, we'll explore what can be done with a compass alone. And that's plenty.

In the North, where lakes can be huge, sprawling, confusing, elaborately sprinkled with islands, bays, and points, and surrounded by low-relief land with few prominent landmarks, you must navigate carefully. You will need a good compass and the knowledge to use it. In addition to compass skills, you will need to develop map and correlation skills.

—Garrett and Alexandra Conover,
The Winter Wilderness Companion

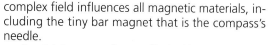

EARTH'S MAGNETIC FIELD

The Chinese are believed to have invented a navigation compass around 2 A.D., and Norse explorers used something similar to reach Iceland in the ninth century. Arab sailors and desert traders began using needles suspended from yarn by the twelfth century. But it wasn't until the 1300s that an instrument we would recognize as a modern compass was developed and commonly used.

Today's compass, even in its simplest form, is a remarkably refined instrument compared with what was in use back then (or even only eighty years ago). Yet, it is still basically the same because it is controlled by something that hasn't changed much—the earth's magnetic field.

Remember in fifth-grade science class how iron filings lined up on a sheet of paper when a bar magnet was placed under it? The filings delineated the magnet's field of force. Well, the earth has the same type of field around it (although it's not as orderly and well organized as the filings), and this complex field influences all magnetic materials, including the tiny bar magnet that is the compass's needle.

Anything magnetic, or affected by magnetism, tries to line itself up with these forces. A compass's needle does not point to some magnetic "mother lode" at each pole, but rather aligns itself with the local magnetic forces flowing around it. That's an important point to remember.

As seen in the drawing, lines of magnetic force run horizontal to the earth's surface near the equator but are nearly perpendicular close to the poles. Therefore, the downward component of the magnetic field—which is called *dip*, or magnetic inclination—varies with location. Only along the *magnetic equator* (ME) does a compass needle lie horizontal. The farther it is from this zone, the more the northern end (or southern, in the Southern Hemisphere) of the needle dips downward.

In extreme cases, the needle dips enough to keep it from swinging properly. To compensate for this, manufacturers counterbalance needles for specific magnetic zones. Compasses sold for use in the United States should be compensated for the zone called *magnetic north* (MN). If you are navigating in a different zone, you need to buy a compass specifically compensated for the region.

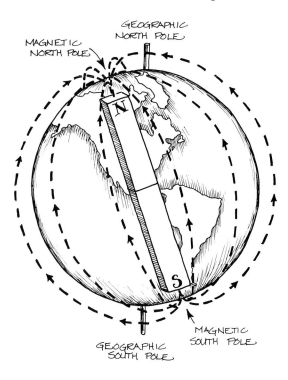

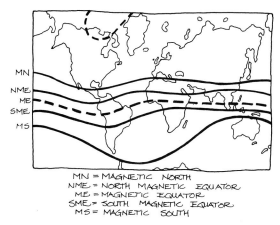

MN = MAGNETIC NORTH
NME = NORTH MAGNETIC EQUATOR
ME = MAGNETIC EQUATOR
SME = SOUTH MAGNETIC EQUATOR
MS = MAGNETIC SOUTH

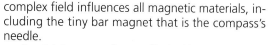

HOW COMPASSES WORK

The workings of a compass could hardly be simpler. The needle pivots in response to the earth's magnetic field and stops when it's aligned with the forces. The needle's northern end then points to an encircling ring marked in degrees, thereby enabling us to determine directions. As we'll see when we investigate the different compass types, there are many variations on this theme. However, this explanation describes how most compasses do their job.

While the workings of a compass are straightforward, there are some fine points of which to be aware. One of your first questions when choosing a compass may be, "How good and accurate an instrument do I need?" The answer is, "One that gives you directions within 2 to 4 degrees. One that is rugged enough to take abuse, compact enough to fit in a pocket, and simple enough to use easily."

Some surveyors' compasses are accurate to within a few minutes (there are 60 minutes in 1 degree), but this is too precise for our needs. Besides, their weight, complexity, delicacy, and cost make them impractical. Because the kind of compass work we'll be doing involves large, easy-to-locate objects (e.g., roads, trails, hills, streams, lakes) rather than pinpoints in the wilderness, 4 degrees of accuracy is sufficient.

One degree of error puts you only about 100 feet off your mark after a 1-mile walk; a 4-degree error puts you off by 400 feet. In any case, the average person can't maintain a compass course to within any less than 2 degrees, and has to work hard to do that.

Spending more money for a compass does not necessarily get you greater accuracy. Anything over $50 is paying for extra options and gadgets, not precision. The desired accuracy can be found in all but the cheapest models (which might still give you a workable 4 degrees). Most of the compasses offered by the manufacturers listed in the appendix do the job.

To be accurate, the needle must be well damped so it doesn't swing about wildly. Most compasses damp excessive motion by having the needle sealed in a case filled with alcohol or light petroleum oil. Test yours by quickly rotating the whole compass 90 degrees; the needle should move no more than 10 degrees and return to north within 3 to 5 seconds. If it swings along with the compass or oscillates back and forth before settling on north, it is poorly damped—making it unreliable and hard to work with in the field.

A small bubble may appear in the liquid at extremely low temperatures (below −40°F or so) or at high altitudes (above 20,000 feet). This will not degrade performance as long as it goes away when conditions return to normal. Do not buy a compass that already has a bubble—the seal may be broken. And do not buy a compass that is pointing in a different direction than all the others in the display case—individuality in a compass is not a positive trait!

As important as accuracy is rugged construction, for no matter how much you try to protect it, your compass will lead a hard life. To make its life easier (and longer), choose one that is compact enough to fit in a shirt or outer pack pocket. You'll also want a compass that is easy to use. Human nature being what it is, what is simple to use gets used the most. The more you refer to your compass and put it to use, the better your chances are of not getting lost.

Certainly my own most memorable hikes can be classified as Shortcuts That Backfired.

—Edward Abbey,
The Journey Home

MAKE YOUR OWN

Be careful with your compass. Hang it by a lanyard around your neck and tuck it under your shirt or in a button-down pocket. If there's room, stow a small backup compass in your pack, or carry a cheap one that hangs from a zipper pull, pins to your shirt, or attaches to a watchband. Everyone in the group should have his or her own. But things happen. You step on your compass, drop it off a cliff, or lose it over the side of the canoe. No need to worry; all is not lost—you can always make your own.

Take any piece of iron or steel that is long, thin, and light. Aluminum or yellow metals won't work; only things that rust will do. A pin or needle is perfect, but a straightened paperclip, piece of steel baling wire or barbed wire, or the clip from a pen (careful, some are chrome or aluminum) could also work.

STRAIGHTENED
PAPER CLIP

ON 2 WOOD CHIPS

Quick-and-dirty makeshift compass needles.

Now, you want that piece of metal to rotate easily. If you are sure that absolutely no drafts will influence it, you can suspend it from a thread. You'll get more reliable results, however, if you float the metal on still water using balled-up paper, a wood chip, or a leaf. Gather some water in a *nonmagnetic* container or a scooped-out recess in the ground, such as a puddle. Resist the temptation to use a "tin" can, which is made of steel (an aluminum can is fine). Place the float on the water, then the metal on it. It will slowly turn to orient itself.

For faster, more positive results, magnetize the metal by rubbing it in one direction with a magnet. Using only one end of the magnet, rub it the length of your compass "needle," lifting the magnet up into the air a few inches after you've reached the end; return to the beginning of the needle before descending for another stroke in the same direction. Keep up this steady circle for six to a dozen strokes and your needle should be well magnetized.

The magnets you are most likely to have with you are those in the speaker or headphones of a radio. Soft steel tends to lose its magnetism fairly quickly, so you might have to remagnetize your needle occasionally, although you shouldn't have to do this more than two or three times in a day.

What if you don't have a magnet? You can improve the direction-finding ability of your pointer by rubbing it (as you would a magnet) with a stone, a piece of silk, or a piece of synthetic material. You can also magnetize it with electrical currents if you happen to have a battery and insulated wire.

Test your compass by disturbing it after it settles. Do this several times; if it returns to the same alignment, you're OK. It will line up north and south, although you have to infer by other means which end is north—use the sun, stars, or any other natural signs in the area. (See chapter 6.)

DECLINATION

In chapter 2, we learned of two norths. The first is geographic north, also known as true north, at one end of the axis around which the earth spins. Mapmakers, by convention, place geographic north at the "top" of the world.

The second is magnetic north, at the northern end of the planet's magnetic core, west of Baffin Island. Maps and charts use geographic north, but the compass is attracted to magnetic north. On land maps, the difference between the two is called *declination*, which varies with your position on the globe.

You need to know the local declination when you want to convert the compass's magnetic readings to a map's geographic directions, or vice versa. But, of course, that need arises only when you use both a map and a compass. When you navigate by compass or map alone, you can ignore declination completely. Nevertheless, the most accurate and dependable way to navigate is to use both, which means that—sooner or later—you need to deal with declination.

Declination is measured in degrees and designated either east (E) or west (W). For example, in New York City, the declination was about 14 degrees west (14° W) in 1994, pulling a compass's magnetized needle to the west of true north by 14 degrees to point at 346 degrees on a properly oriented geographic scale.

In San Diego, the declination was about 14 degrees east (14° E) in 1994, pulling a compass needle 14 degrees east of true north to read 014 degrees on the geographic scale.

There are places where declination is greater, places where it is less, and places (e.g., parts of Michigan, Indiana, Ohio, Kentucky, Tennessee, and North and South Carolina) where it doesn't exist at all. You can see where by looking at an *isogonic* (i.e., equal-angle) *chart*.

The lines on an isogonic chart connect points of equal angles of declination, just as contour lines connect points of equal altitude. As you can see, the pattern of magnetic forces is not particularly orderly—not at all like the neatly regimented iron filings in the fifth-grade bar-magnet experiment. Note the *agonic* (i.e., no-angle) lines where there is no declination at all; at these spots, magnetic north coincides with geographic north.

The earth's magnetic field is not only irregular, it also moves, creeping slowly westward. For example, the agonic (0 declination) line that is now west of Florida went through the center of that peninsula in 1970. This movement is called the *annual westward change*.

But don't let all this daunt you; it's not as chaotic as it might seem. To find your local declination, all you have to do is look at the declination diagram on your topographical map. There, too, you usually find the annual westward change—which in most places is an increase or decrease of only a few minutes per year. To see if you have to make corrections for the annual change, look in the legend to find the year the map was compiled.

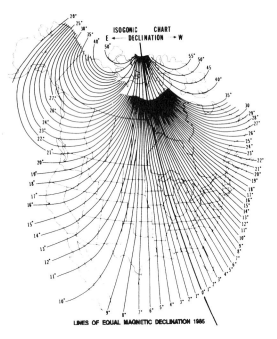

Isogonic map of Canada and the United States.
COURTESY BRUNTON

If it was some years ago, you might have to calculate the change in declination since then.

Don't ever be misled into believing you can ignore declination. It's sometimes natural to wish the compass needle were pointing to true north, but wishing won't make it so. There are parts of Alaska where declination is so great—more than 24° E on the western end of the North Slope—that if you didn't adjust for it, you'd find yourself more than a third of a mile off course after a 1-mile walk. Even just a few degrees of declination, when combined with compass inaccuracies and reading errors, can get you into trouble. And if you are making a long trip, check each new map's declination as you go. It will change slightly, especially if your route runs east or west.

When using a compass with a map, you must compensate for the effect of declination. This can be done arithmetically, by adding or subtracting the declination; by adjusting the compass's bearing ring to read geographic rather than magnetic north; or by drawing magnetic north–south reference lines on the map. The particulars of these techniques are explained in chapter 4.

If you don't know the current local declination and your map or trail guide isn't telling you, you can measure it. Take a compass bearing from one mapped object to another, then compare your reading with the bearing on the map. The difference between the two is the local declination—provided you weren't holding your compass near a metal canteen when you took the bearing!

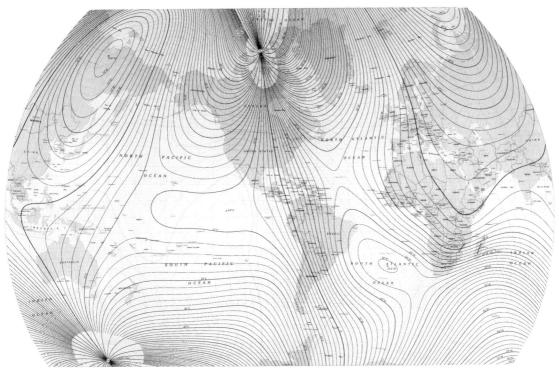

Isogonic map of the world.

COMPASS TYPES

The Baseplate Compass

This is often called an *orienteering compass* because it was invented in 1928 by Gunnar Tillander, an unemployed instrument maker in Sweden, who made it for the sport of orienteering, in which contestants use a map and compass to seek out a series of landmarks as quickly as possible. A baseplate compass has made navigating so much easier that it has since been adopted as the standard for wilderness travel, and is now the most common type available from outdoor suppliers.

It is nothing more than a simple fixed-dial compass (explained later) mounted so that it rotates on a transparent baseplate. The rotating case is marked in 2- or 5-degree increments running clockwise around its dial. The clear center portion of the case has north–south orienting lines, as well as an orienting arrow that makes it easy to align the needle with the "N" mark (north).

What makes the baseplate compass so practical is that it gives you a choice of indicating directions either with or without the use of numbered degrees. The base doubles as a protractor for determining bearings from a map, and its edges are inscribed with map scales or a ruler to measure map distances. Almost all include an adjustment you can use to compensate for declination, converting magnetic bearings to geographic bearings that can be used directly with a map.

Other nice but unnecessary features are a magnifier to help read small map details, a *clinometer* to see how steep a slope is, and a sighting mirror, which is a flip-up mirror with a vertical line inscribed down its center. You raise the mirror, hold the compass so the line on the mirror crosses the needle's pivot point, look across the notched sight, and read the dial's reflection where the mirror's line crosses it.

A baseplate compass is simple to use, easy to refer to in the field, extremely versatile, and relatively inexpensive—which is why it should be your first choice when purchasing a compass. For these reasons, much of the information presented later in this book presumes the use of a baseplate compass.

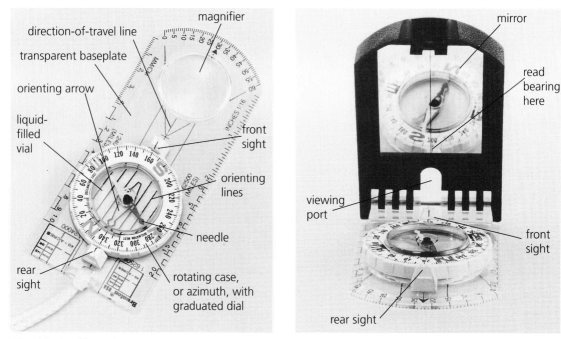

Two kinds of baseplate compasses.

The Fixed-Dial Compass

This is the simplest compass. A needle is free to pivot on a bearing and rotate within a case marked in degrees running clockwise around its circumference. It is a good basic tool and, because there is not much to it, it tends to be cheaper than other compass types. However, it is not used for serious navigation.

A fixed-dial compass is hard to read with accuracy, so it is not wise to spend a lot of money on one. Admittedly, people found their way through the great unknown for centuries with this type of compass. But then there was no alternative, and there are no statistics on the number of navigators who got lost. Today, other compasses are more versatile and easier to use. If you already have a fixed-dial compass, by all means, use it. Better yet, take it along in your pack as a backup for the more practical baseplate compass.

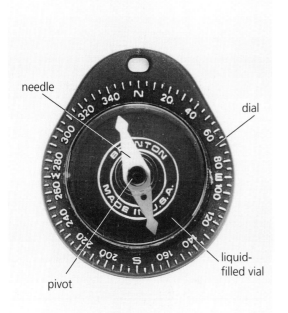

An inexpensive fixed-dial compass that hangs from a zipper pull.

The Magnetic-Card Compass

The classic compass, as seen in the previous two examples, has a needle free to rotate on its pivot around a fixed dial. However, in the magnetic-card compass, needle and dial are joined (on a card) to rotate as one unit. The advantage is that "N" (north) on the card is always aligned with magnetic north, so there are no extra steps needed to orient the compass before taking a reading. The disadvantage is that you can't compensate for declination. Conversions from magnetic readings to geographic, or back, must be done by arithmetic (instructions are in the appendix).

If all your route-finding is done with a compass alone and no maps, the magnetic-card type works quite well. The most common examples of this type are the military-style compass with a small lens to magnify the reading and compasses sold for use in boats or automobiles.

The military compass has forward and rear sights for aiming the instrument. You look through the sights at a landmark, then through the lens to read the bearing indicated by the *lubber line*, which is a mark on the forward part of the case in line with the sights. It is thought to have gotten its unusual name in the early days of sailing ships, when sailors thought only a lubber (i.e., clumsy oaf) needed this forward-pointing line to guide a vessel. The purpose of the sights and the lens is to improve bearing accuracy. Compared with baseplate compasses, this type is not as versatile, can't be easily used with a map, and is only theoretically more accurate, which

> What is it that makes it so hard sometimes to determine whither we will walk? I believe that there is a subtle magnetism in Nature, which, if we unconsciously yield to it, will direct us aright.
>
> —Henry David Thoreau, "Walking"

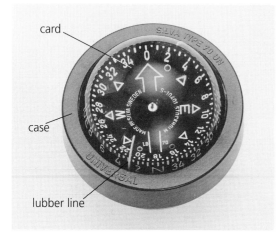

Automobile and marine compass.

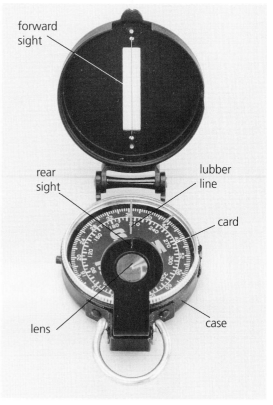

Military-style lensatic compass.

is why outdoor equipment suppliers rarely stock them. They are usually found in military surplus outlets. If you already have one, by all means, learn its ways and use it.

Marine and automobile magnetic-card compasses are ideal for use in almost any vehicle: boats, snowmobiles, trucks, even dogsleds. No matter which direction the vehicle is pointing, the lubber line shows that bearing. All you have to do is mount the compass so you can view the lubber line directly, and so that the central pivot of the compass and the lubber line are parallel to the vehicle's centerline. This ensures that both compass and vehicle point in the same direction.

Any compass mounted near ferrous metals or electrical currents will be erratic. In a car, or wherever these potentially disturbing influences are found, the compass deviates from its alignment with the earth's magnetic field. In all but the cheapest boat or car compass, this deviation can be compensated for—partially if not completely—with adjustable internal magnets.

ORIENTING YOUR COMPASS TO MAGNETIC NORTH

1. The Baseplate Compass

With the orienting arrow pointing to "N" (north) on the case's dial, hold the baseplate and then rotate the case so the needle is enclosed within the orienting arrow's outline. The compass is now oriented to magnetic north and directions can be read from where the direction-of-travel line intersects the case's dial.

2. The Fixed-Dial Compass

The premise of this compass's operation is that the needle always stays aligned with magnetic north. The north end of the needle is painted red, striped, marked with an N, or shaped like an arrowhead. Once the needle has settled in position, turn the whole compass so the printed N (north, or 360 degrees) on the dial comes under the north end of the needle. The compass is now oriented to magnetic north and directions can be read from it.

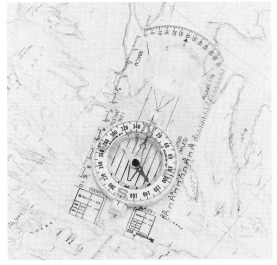

Baseplate compass needle and orienting arrow out of alignment.

3. The Magnetic-Card Compass

This compass is always aligned with magnetic north and no extra steps are needed before taking a bearing.

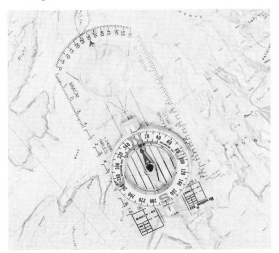

Baseplate compass needle aligned with orienting arrow. The compass sits on a Trails Illustrated map of Zion National Park.

A fixed-dial compass oriented to magnetic north. The bearing of any visible object can now be read from the dial. The Canadian topo covers a piece of Ontario east of Georgian Bay.

ORIENTING YOUR COMPASS TO GEOGRAPHIC NORTH

1. The Baseplate Compass

One of the nicest features of a baseplate compass is that almost all of them can be adjusted to compensate for declination. The method is different for each manufacturer, but the principle is the same. The clear center portion of the case, with the north–south orienting lines and arrow, can be rotated within the case's outer dial.

When you purchase the compass, the orienting arrow is pointing to N, so the compass reads magnetic directions. But if you rotate the center of the case so the orienting arrow is offset from N by the amount of your local declination, the compass reads in geographic directions.

All you are doing is moving the magnetic north indicator to coincide with its true bearing. Now when you read the compass, it will be in directions that relate to those on a map, with no need to bother further about declination.

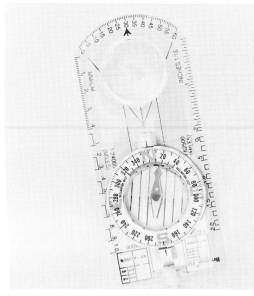

Baseplate compass oriented to geographic north in a place (e.g., San Diego in 1994) where the declination is 14 degrees east . . .

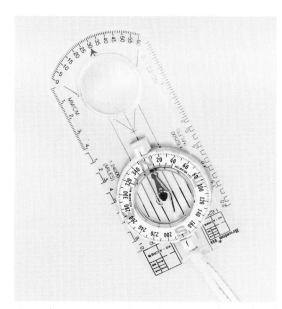

Baseplate compass oriented to magnetic north. All readings are in degrees magnetic.

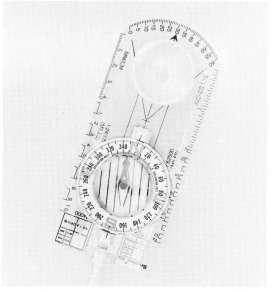

. . . and in a place (e.g., New York City in 1994) where it is 14 degrees west. In both cases, all readings are in "true" or "map" degrees.

Fixed-dial compass oriented to geographic north where the local declination is 14 degrees east . . .

2. The Fixed-Dial Compass

When using this compass with a map, you have to correct for declination. One way is by addition or subtraction. It's simple enough, but if you tend to become confused, especially at times of stress, you don't need to bother with it. This is explained in the appendix for those who are interested.

An easier way to compensate for declination is by putting a mark or piece of tape on the case. When the needle points to the mark, the compass is oriented to geographic north. For example, with 14 degrees west declination, put the mark 14 degrees west of the dial's north (at 346 degrees). With 14 degrees east declination, put the mark 14 degrees east of the dial's north (at 014 degrees).

3. The Magnetic-Card Compass

With this compass, there's no physical way to compensate for declination. To convert its magnetic readings to true or geographic bearings, you have no option but to use simple arithmetic.

. . . and where it is 14 degrees west. All readings are in "true" or "map" degrees.

BEARINGS

A bearing is the direction of one object from another, measured as a horizontal angle from a fixed baseline. In our case, that baseline is either true north or magnetic north. When taking a bearing with a baseplate compass or a fixed-dial compass, always hold it straight in front of you; looking at it from the side does not give you a correct reading. On compasses with an optional direction-of-travel arrow, this manually set pointer is used as a memory aid to mark the desired bearing on the dial. All compass work is based on three types of bearings.

Direct Bearings

Whether or not you know your position, a compass tells you the direction toward a landmark you can identify on the map. For example, "The compass shows that the tower bears 060 degrees from my position." (Incidentally, to avoid confusion, careful navigators always use the three-digit notation with bearings.) Here's how you can measure that bearing with your compass.

1. The Baseplate Compass
Hold the compass level at your waist or chest and in your left hand (if you're right-handed). Point the direction-of-travel line at the landmark. Turn the case with your right hand until the orienting arrow is aligned with the north end of needle. Read the bearing where the direction-of-travel line intersects the case's dial.

2. The Fixed-Dial Compass
Face the landmark. Hold the compass level in both hands at your waist or chest, making "pointers" with your two index fingers. Aim at the landmark. Orient the compass by rotating it between your fingers until the needle points to "N". Read the direct bearing in degrees on the far side of the dial along an imaginary line connecting the pivot and the landmark.

3. The Magnetic-Card Compass
Look straight at the lubber line; sighting at an angle gives an incorrect reading. Extend an imaginary line from the central pivot through the lubber line to the landmark. The bearing is read where the lubber line intersects the card.

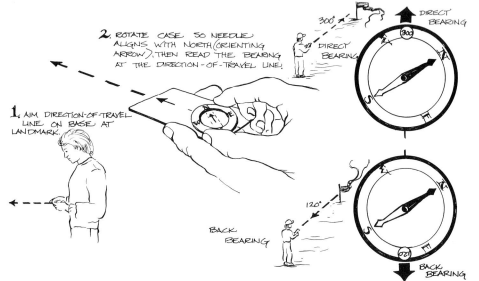

Use of baseplate compass to take direct and back bearings.

Reciprocal or "Back" Bearings

When you don't know your exact position, a compass tells you the direction from a landmark to where you stand (which is the *reciprocal*, or dead opposite, of the direct bearing). For example, "My position bears 240 degrees from that tower." Here's how to do it with your compass.

1. The Baseplate Compass

Hold the compass level at your waist or chest and in your left hand (if you're right-handed). Point the direction-of-travel line at the landmark. Turn the case with your right hand until the orienting arrow is aligned with the south end of the needle. Read the back bearing where the direction-of-travel line intersects the case's dial.

Because a back bearing is the exact opposite of a direct bearing, it differs from it by 180 degrees; therefore, it's simple to calculate one from the other. If the direct bearing you observe is 180 degrees or greater, subtract 180 degrees to get the back bearing. If the direct bearing is less than 180 degrees, add 180 degrees to the direct bearing to get the back bearing.

2. The Fixed-Dial Compass

Follow the steps for taking a direct bearing. Read the back bearing in degrees on the near side of the dial along the extension of an imaginary line connecting the pivot and the landmark. Or, after the direct bearing has been taken, rotate the compass so the north end of the needle points to the degree notation of the direct bearing instead of to north (N). The south end of the needle indicates the back bearing.

Once again, you can easily calculate a back bearing. If the direct bearing is greater than 180 degrees, subtract 180 degrees to get the back bearing. If the direct bearing is less than 180 degrees, add 180 to get the back bearing.

Use of fixed-dial compass to take direct and back bearings.

3. The Magnetic-Card Compass

Take a direct bearing as explained previously. If the direct bearing is greater than 180 degrees, subtract 180 degrees to get the back bearing. If the direct bearing is less than 180 degrees, add 180 degrees to get the back bearing.

Finding a Landmark

You can locate a landmark by sighting along a known bearing. For example, "I should be able to find the tower on a bearing of 060 degrees." Here's how to do it with your compass.

1. The Baseplate Compass

Turn the case's dial so the bearing to be set coincides with the direction-of-travel line. Hold the compass level with both hands at your waist or chest. Turn your whole body until the orienting arrow is aligned with the north end of the needle. Look along the direction-of-travel line to find the landmark.

2. The Fixed-Dial compass

Hold the compass level in both hands at your waist or chest, making "pointers" with your two index fingers. The pointers should be an extension of an imaginary line connecting the pivot and the known bearing on the dial. Turn your whole body until the compass is oriented with the needle pointing to "N". Look in the direction of the pointers to find the landmark.

3. The Magnetic-Card Compass

Point the compass so that the desired bearing lies on the lubber line. To find the landmark, sight along an imaginary line from the central pivot through the lubber line.

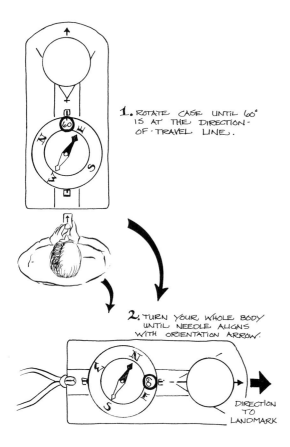

Finding a 60° bearing with a baseplate compass.

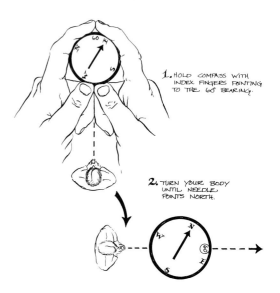

Finding a 60° bearing with a fixed-dial compass.

DEVIATION

The earth's magnetic field is not a particularly powerful force—you won't find it lining up your refrigerator magnets every morning. So the magnetic needle, or card, of a compass has to be very sensitive—enough that it can be unintentionally deflected from its natural alignment by everyday objects. Keep your compass away from radios, knives, belt buckles (even those that look like brass), cameras, battery-powered watches, guns, overhead power lines, and railroad tracks. And never put it on the hood of your car to do map work!

Any irregular influence that overrides the natural magnetic field is called *deviation*. It's a good idea to check for deviation before heading out. Do this with your full pack on and holding the compass as you would on the trail. When using a map, take bearings from a known position to identifiable landmarks. When at an unknown position, use transits, as described previously. Correct for declination and see if the compass's readings match those from the map. If you have no map, check your bearings against someone else's compass—or use the North Star or the sun (see chapter 6). If your bearings seem weird, look for deviation.

Areas of serious magnetic disturbance are usually marked on maps and nautical charts. On land, there are many places where magnetic anomalies occur—in mountainous or hilly terrain and in other areas—because of ore deposits. In northern latitudes, watch out for "bog iron" in or near large, flat heath-bog terrain. These deposits may throw a compass off by many degrees.

Beware, too, of deviation that you introduce yourself—apart from the belt buckles and radios already mentioned. Think about what's fairly near your compass when you take a sight—in your backpack, maybe. Metal flashlights and batteries are notorious for affecting compasses. Beware of the ferrous metal in your eyeglass frames when you hold a compass to your eye. And if you have a pacemaker—well, you might just have to ask someone else to take the sight for you.

Compensating for Deviation

There is no need to compensate a handheld compass. If it doesn't seem right, step a few feet to one side or put it down so you are not holding it. The deviation should disappear.

Although I prefer to navigate with just a map, I always carry a compass. For trail travel, I hardly ever need it, except perhaps when at an unsigned junction in thick mist or dense forest. For cross-country walking, though, a compass may prove essential, especially when visibility is poor.

—Chris Townsend,
The Backpacker's Handbook

FOLLOWING A COMPASS COURSE

Part 1. Going Straight

A compass helps you maintain a straight course toward an objective, even if you lose sight of your objective along the way. You need its help because you can't walk a straight course on your own. As we discussed in chapter 1, people tend to veer off in a circle (usually clockwise) when they are cut off from sensory reference. This can happen in snow, fog, rain, darkness, or in a thick forest. Even if you think you'll be able to see your destination at all times, use a compass anyway—be prepared.

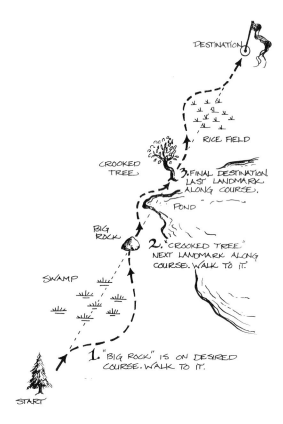

Divide long trips into short segments. Choose landmarks that will not be obscured, and try to keep your intermediate goal and starting point in view as you walk.

A good example of when this might be necessary is passing through thick woods to reach a destination that is obscured from view most of the way. It seems that all you have to do is take a bearing of your destination at the start and then follow that heading on the compass, but it's not that easy.

First, take the bearing toward your objective. Write it down so you won't forget it or, when using a baseplate compass, be careful not to rotate the case and accidentally move the orienting arrow. Once you have the bearing, don't just set off in that direction. Look ahead to the limit of your vision and choose a distinctive intermediate landmark on that same bearing. Then put the compass away and walk to the landmark. Before you go, however, find or make a recognizable landmark at the spot you are leaving so that you can check your course by referring back to your starting place.

If you try to watch the compass while you're walking, you'll wind up stepping off a cliff or sustaining world-class shin damage from tripping over logs. Just walk to your chosen intermediate landmark by the easiest route—it doesn't have to be straight. Once there, take out the compass and sight along your original bearing to find the next intermediate landmark, and walk to that. Proceed in small steps, checking yourself along the way while heading on your original bearing. Repeat this procedure until you've reached your destination.

Part 2. Lateral Drift

The reason for making a series of short jumps instead of one long compass run is lateral drift. A compass bearing without a visible destination gives you only forward direction and, using only a bearing, you have no way of knowing if you have strayed to one side or the other of it. This is why it is so important to maintain visual contact with both your starting point and an intermediate landmark.

But what happens when you lose sight of your intermediate landmark? To check if you are still headed toward it, take a back bearing from where you are to the spot you just left (this is why it is important to mark or remember your last position). If the back bearing is not 180 degrees from your original bearing, walk to one side or the other until it is.

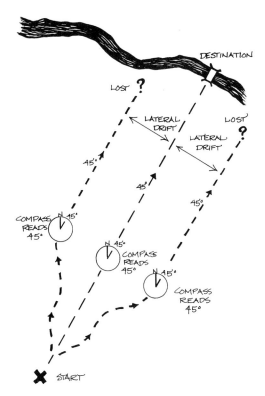

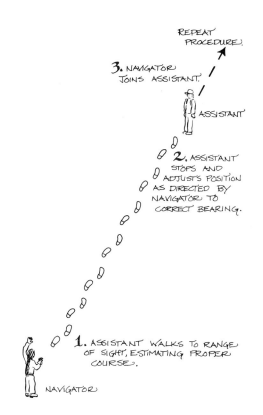

Then turn around and sight ahead along the original bearing; your intermediate landmark should be off in that direction.

Don't just keep plowing ahead on your original bearing after losing the landmark. Lateral drift may have occurred. The compass assures you that you are on the correct bearing. However, there is an infinite number of similar bearings all lying parallel to each other, with only one connecting your starting point and the landmark. The only way to find that one is by taking a back bearing.

Part 3. Without Landmarks

Although it is not likely, there may come a time in flat, open country when no intermediate landmarks can be found. You can see your destination far off in the haze, but if darkness, the weather, or anything else blocks it from view, you could be in trouble. When nature doesn't provide landmarks, ingenuity is needed.

One way to be sure you proceed in a straight line is to make your own transit. When two widely spaced objects appear to line up, you know you are on an extension of the line (i.e., the transit) that connects them. But please do not erect transit markers that you leave behind, such as a *cairn* (i.e., pile of rocks) or a branch stuck in the ground with a scrap of cloth on it. The proliferation of "bad cairns" is a problem in many parks and wilderness areas, and they are often the reason inexperienced parties get lost because they were built by people who were themselves "lost." A marker that involves litter is doubly harmful.

If you're with a group, send someone ahead to the limit of your vision on the desired bearing. Use hand signals and your compass set with the bearing to position the person as a human intermediate landmark. Your human marker then double-checks with a back bearing. When all is set, your marker stays put, you join your partner, and then start the process over again.

It's also possible to hold a reasonably straight course for a short distance, even if you have no compass and can't see any landmarks. By having at least three people walking in single file and spaced far apart, the last member of the group can see if the lead is veering off course. Don't count on it for too long, though. If the last person goes off course, or even the middle one, the whole group will go astray.

There may not be a single wilderness in the lower forty-eight states, and no more than a very few in Alaska and Canada, that is featureless enough to require artificial transits. If you're traveling solo over a featureless landscape, you may wish to take along a GPS receiver (see chapter 8). Don't leave a trail of blazes, cairns, or other markings behind you.

Part 4. Around Obstacles

Sometimes you head off on a straight course and encounter an unforeseen obstacle. Whether it's a precipice, rough ground, a bog, or a field of nasty-looking bulls, you'll have to find your way around it without being thrown off course. There are two variations on this situation.

In the first, you can see where you want to go but can't walk directly to it. A river blocks your way and the only place to ford it is far upstream. Or maybe your course would take you through a poison-ivy patch. The solution is to use an intermediate landmark.

Find a marker where you stop, look to the other side of the obstacle for an intermediate landmark that is on your course, and then get to it any way you can. Confirm that you have reached the landmark and that it is on your course with a back bearing to your starting point. When there is no obvious landmark on the opposite side, you either have to send someone around to act as a human landmark or, if you're alone, go around and take back bearings on the starting point until you regain your course.

In the other variation, you can't see across or through whatever is in your way—a hill, a dense swamp, or fog on a lake. The only way to pick up

WALK EQUAL NUMBER OF PACES ON 120° AND 300° COURSES.

COMPASS BASE TURNED SIDEWAYS

START

your bearing on the other side is to make a detour with a series of short, right-angle legs. Here's how.

Turn 90 degrees from your course and walk until you are clear of the obstruction, counting your steps as you go. Then turn 90 degrees back onto the original course and continue walking (no need to count steps this time). Turn 90 degrees once more, this time walking back toward your base course line, counting out the same number of steps as you did on the first leg. The lengths of the two "out" and "back" legs must be equal, which is why keeping track of the number of steps you take is important.

This technique can be done with any compass by adding or subtracting the 90 degrees; however, it is a lot easier if you use a baseplate compass. Without moving the orienting arrow and keeping the needle in place, sight along the back edge on the leg out and the leg back. This automatically gives you 90-degree turns, with no chance of losing or forgetting your original course.

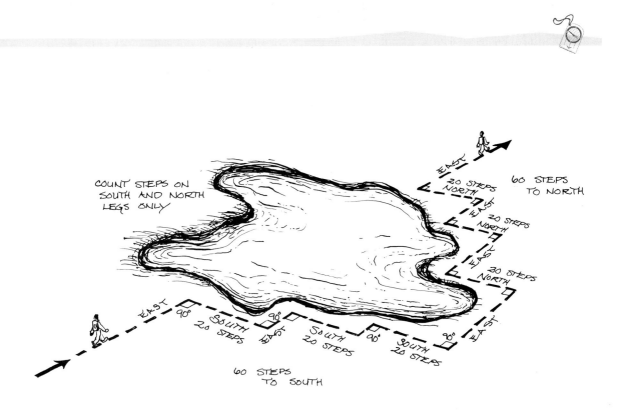

COUNT STEPS ON
SOUTH AND NORTH
LEGS ONLY

EAST
20 STEPS
NORTH

60 STEPS
TO NORTH

EAST
90° SOUTH
20 STEPS

SOUTH
20 STEPS

SOUTH
20 STEPS

60 STEPS
TO SOUTH

Facts Don't Lie

There are times when we must tell stories about ourselves, even though it might hurt. This embarrassing incident happened while I was working as a wilderness ranger in New Mexico with my wife. It imparts a lesson from which everyone can learn. For brevity, I'll recount only the fraction of this epic afternoon patrol that applies to this chapter.

I'll start on top of Latir Mesa, where my wife and I reunited after having separated in a driving thunderstorm that was still raging around us. I, of course, with no rain gear on hand, was ill-prepared for the sudden squall and got drenched —and cold. We headed out on what we *thought* was the route over the mesa that would loop us

back to camp. I looked at the map and the compass but ignored what they were telling me, following my hypothermic intuition. A short while later, I again checked the map and started us on a backtrack route that was, in fact, the correct way to go. Then I second-guessed my correct second guess and turned us around again, heading back into the storm.

We crested a rise and looked down at a lake. Although the compass indicated that the lake lay in the wrong direction, I was convinced it was the one we had set as our destination—almost home free. Descending hundreds of feet, we passed by the lake and began to follow the outlet stream that didn't look like anything I remembered.

Jumping and scrambling down a steep-walled little canyon, I began to get a sinking feeling. I pulled the map and compass out once again. This time, I actually took into account the facts and realized we were not anywhere near where we wanted to be. It was the compass pointing north that finally convinced me we were headed to Colorado and not back to camp. With that, we dug down into our reserves, climbed back up and over Latir Mesa, and got back to camp in the stumbling darkness, much wiser than when we had left.

PJC

TESTING YOUR SKILLS

The difference between thinking we can do something by just reading about it and actually doing it is always greater than we expect. As easy as compass work is—and it is easy—it still won't be anything like what you thought it would be when the time comes to turn knowledge into action.

Now is the time, before it becomes a matter of either getting home or spending the night lost, to come to terms with your compass. Learn how you interact with it and read it. See what its idiosyncrasies are, and yours. Pick up your compass and this book, find an open field, and do these exercises:

Checking back bearings.

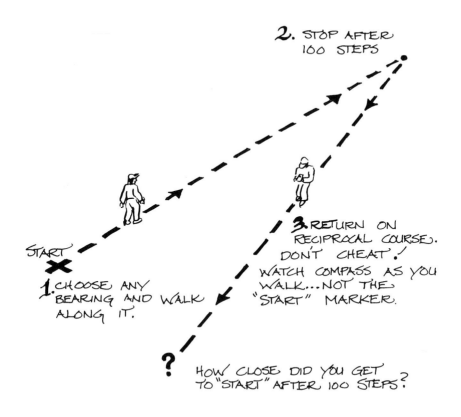

Out-and-back accuracy.

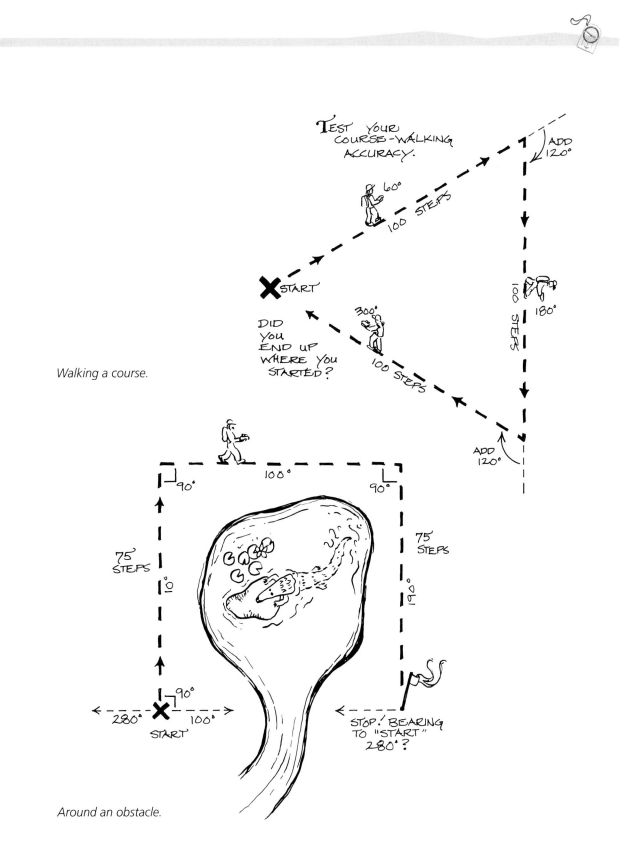

TEST YOUR COURSE-WALKING ACCURACY.

ADD 120°

60°

100 STEPS

X START

DID YOU END UP WHERE YOU STARTED?

300°

100 STEPS

100 STEPS

180°

ADD 120°

Walking a course.

90°

100°

90°

75 STEPS

0°

75 STEPS

190°

90°

280°

100°

START

STOP! BEARING TO "START" 280°?

Around an obstacle.

Having become familiar with maps and compasses, we are ready to combine them, merging the two into something called *navigation*. It's a big jump and a definite improvement over being just a map-reader or compass-user. The principles of navigation are easy to acquire and simple to apply and, once grasped, they make getting lost more difficult than staying found. Navigation is about motion. It's the ability to travel without getting disoriented. While surveying or position-finding gives you your immediate location, navigation not only tells you where you are, but also where you've been, where you will be, how to get there, when you'll get there, and how to get back. It's based on a common universal reference: north. No matter where you go, north stays put. With a compass and map aligned toward north, you have an almost foolproof way of staying oriented. And that is what this chapter is about: the use of map and compass to keep track of your ever-changing position as you travel through the wilderness.

Of course, there is the problem of having two norths—one geographic, the other magnetic. You have to choose one on which to base your navigation. But this, too, is simple. You can use either one, choosing whichever best suits your needs.

With that in mind, and map and compass in hand, we begin a series of bearing-taking techniques, matching directions between map and compass. You'll choose a direction on the map and convert it to a course you can follow on the compass. Bearings also are used to locate an object whose only proof of existence is a mark on the map—or the other way around, to find on the map what you see in front of you. Then there are special bearings—*lines of position*—that tell you where you are when you haven't got a clue. Lines of position can pinpoint you on the map, let you return to that same place, and keep you out of danger. Finally, we provide some helpful esoterica about distance—how far you've gone and how far you still have to go—and how that's used to keep track of where you are.

After reading this chapter, you'll be able to find your way out and back from almost anywhere in the world. If you were worried before, you should no longer have any fear of getting lost. This fear (which exists to some degree in all of us) can, in extreme cases, keep you from exploring new places and stifle the spirit of adventure, which—if you've read this far—is probably a significant part of your nature. Soon you'll have what it takes to get out there and enjoy the wilderness with one less thing to worry about.

MAP AND COMPASS COMBINED

Choosing a Point of Reference

To navigate successfully, you must choose one reference point and relate all directions to it. By convention and for convenience, we use north as that point—either geographic or magnetic.

Maps are based on geographic north. The vertical lines of longitude that run up and down the map connect the geographic north and south poles. When you derive a direction from a map, the course is given in reference to geographic north.

Compasses, on the other hand, use magnetic north, which can vary from geographic north by as much as 21 degrees in the contiguous United States and even more in Canada and Alaska. The difference between the two norths, as we learned earlier, is called *declination* on land maps and *variation* on nautical charts.

Now, let's assume you're at a trail junction in a fog-shrouded valley in Colorado. The map says that by traveling toward 270 degrees, you will find a cabin 2 miles away. If you simply walked on a course of 270 degrees according to your compass, you'd miss the cabin by more than 2,500 feet and probably wander around with growing apprehension until the fog lifted. That's because you ignored the 13 degrees of east declination relevant to this area, which is the difference between magnetic (compass) and geographic (map) directions. And that's why maps and compasses can't "talk" to each other without some translation.

Except in the few parts of the world where there is no declination, you must choose one reference point—the map's or the compass's—and translate the other to it. In navigating, you can speak either "compass" or "map," but trying to use both at once guarantees that you will soon be lost.

Your choice defines the system of navigation on which you will rely. Once the selection is made for a particular journey, stay with it, or confusion and disorientation will reign. Each system has advantages and disadvantages, as we're about to see. But most serious navigators use geographic, or true, north because the map is the primary tool. As a result, they habitually correct their compass readings for declination.

Geographic, or True, North

If you decide to use the map's geographic north as your point of reference, as most wilderness navigators do, your compass readings need to be corrected to match it. You can do this either arithmetically or by making the compass read as if it were pointing to geographic rather than magnetic north.

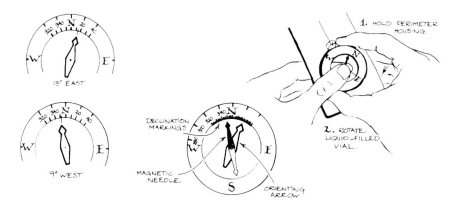

Declination adjustment in a baseplate compass. When the needle aligns with the offset orienting arrow, the compass reads to geographic north.

Advantages

Adapting the compass to the map, rather than the other way around, is the easiest way to compensate for declination. It is especially easy with a baseplate (i.e., orienteering) type of compass that has a built-in declination adjustment feature. Set your local declination and then forget about it; from then on, the compass automatically reads geographic north.

Disadvantages

There aren't many. The declination-adjustment feature on a baseplate compass adds a few dollars to the cost. The tape used on a fixed-dial compass can shift or fall off.

Making the Compass Read Geographic North

There are two ways. To use either, you should look up your declination in the legend of a local map, correcting as necessary for the annual change in declination since your map was printed (see chapter 3).

The first way is to use simple arithmetic. You can convert from magnetic to geographic by adding or subtracting the declination from what you read on the compass or find on the map. This technique is explained in the appendix. While the

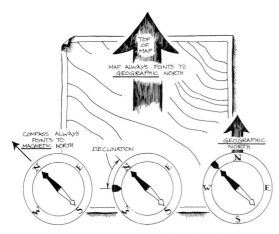

Declination adjustment in a fixed-dial compass. When the needle points to the tape, the compass reads to geographic north.

rules are not difficult, they can be confusing, especially when you're hurried or anxious.

The faster and more reliable way is to offset your compass. You can reposition north on the compass by the same amount as the declination. When the needle points to your new north instead of to the inscribed N on the dial, all directions become relative to geographic north. (See chapter 3 for more information.)

Magnetic North

If you decide to use the compass's magnetic north as your point of reference, then the directions found on a map need to be corrected to match it. You can do this either mathematically or by drawing lines on the map that are aligned with magnetic north.

Advantages

You can use any type of compass, with no need to buy a baseplate compass or resort to tape on a fixed-dial compass face.

Disadvantages

It's cumbersome to convert a map to magnetic north. You have to inscribe parallel lines that are at the same angle and direction as the declination. The process requires a large flat surface, pencil, protractor, and ruler. It takes time and care, and it's almost impossible to accomplish on the trail. The procedure must be repeated for every map you need.

Making the Map Read Magnetic North

There are two ways. To use either, you have to know your local declination, which can be found in the map's legend—adjusted for the annual change in declination.

You can convert from geographic to magnetic by adding or subtracting the declination from what you read on the compass or find on the map. This technique is explained in the appendix.

You can also convert the map. This requires you to draw lines aligned to magnetic north. All map directions can then be oriented to those magnetic lines, making them compatible with readings from a compass.

You could draw lines over the whole map, but that would require a lot of work and the use of a yardstick to draw such long lines. A more practical alternative is to draw lines on only the sections you will use. You can do this with a 12-inch ruler that fits in your pack. You'll also need a pencil and a plastic protractor with a 6-inch ruler (which could substitute for the 12-inch ruler if space is at a premium) on the bottom. Here's how to proceed:

1. Connect the fine, black latitude marks on the left and right borders of the map. This gives you four horizontal lines: the two lines you just drew and the top and bottom borders.
2. Note the declination in the map's legend.
3. Mark a point on one of the horizontal lines near where you will be traveling or taking bearings.
4. Place the protractor on the marked point and measure out the declination angle. Refer to the declination diagram to see which way MN inclines. Do not use the indicators on the declination diagram to measure the angle, use only the written degree values. The angular difference between the magnetic and geographic north indicators is only symbolic; it is not accurate.
5. Using a ruler, extend the angle as far as possible or necessary.
6. Draw lines parallel to the first, using the width of the ruler.

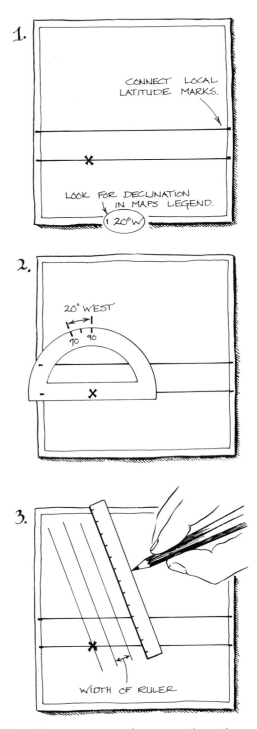

Preparing a map to read to magnetic north.

ORIENTING THE MAP WITH A COMPASS

In chapter 2, you learned how to orient (align) a map to the surrounding landscape by comparing identifiable features in the field with those on the map, and then turning the map until it related to what you saw. But if you're not sure what landmarks you're looking at, or when there are no landmarks, you'll have to use a compass.

The map-and-compass exercises in this chapter are demonstrated with a baseplate compass. It makes most procedures much faster and simpler.

Compass Corrected for Declination

1. The compass's declination adjustment is already offset to correspond with geographic north.
2. Rotate the compass's dial so that north (N, or 360 degrees) is at the direction-of-travel line.
3. Place the baseplate along the map's right- or left-hand border. The direction-of-travel line must be toward the top of the map.
4. Turn the map, with the compass on it, until the needle is enclosed within the orienting arrow's outline. The map is now oriented with the landscape.

Map Corrected for Declination

1. You've already drawn lines on the map that correspond to magnetic north.
2. Rotate the compass's dial so that north (N, or 360 degrees) is at the direction-of-travel line.
3. Place the baseplate along one of the MN lines drawn on the map. The direction-of-travel line must be toward the top of the map.
4. Turn the map, with the compass on it, until the needle is enclosed within the orienting arrow's outline. The map is now oriented.

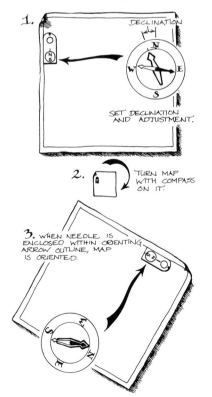

1. DECLINATION

SET DECLINATION AND ADJUSTMENT.

2. TURN MAP WITH COMPASS ON IT.

3. WHEN NEEDLE IS ENCLOSED WITHIN ORIENTING ARROW OUTLINE, MAP IS ORIENTED.

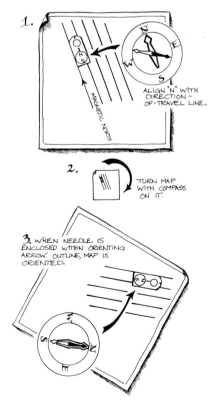

1. MAGNETIC NORTH

ALIGN "N" WITH DIRECTION-OF-TRAVEL LINE.

2. TURN MAP WITH COMPASS ON IT.

3. WHEN NEEDLE IS ENCLOSED WITHIN ORIENTING ARROW OUTLINE, MAP IS ORIENTED.

FINDING A COURSE FROM THE MAP

This assumes that you know where you and your objective are on the map, and now need a compass course to use in the field. From the map, you can determine the direction to your destination, correct for declination, and then follow your compass.

This is the job that the baseplate compass was invented for and does best. Previously, we saw how to use a protractor to find directions on a map. Because a baseplate compass takes the place of a protractor, you now have one less piece of equipment to carry. Furthermore, once the direction is dialed into the compass, it stays locked in place to be used as a bearing in the field. The baseplate compass combines protractor, compass, and ruler into one tool.

Compass Corrected for Declination

1. Set the compass's declination adjustment.
2. Connect your position and objective with a course line that intersects one of the map's vertical borders or a line of longitude.
3. Place the compass's baseplate along the course line and its transparent case over a vertical line. The baseplate can be and usually is used to link position and objective.

4. Rotate the case until north and south on the dial (not the orienting arrow!) are parallel to the vertical line. For now, ignore the needle.
5. The course is shown where the direction-of-travel line intersects the dial.
6. Hold the compass in front of you and turn your whole body until the needle is enclosed within the orienting arrow's outline. Follow that course.

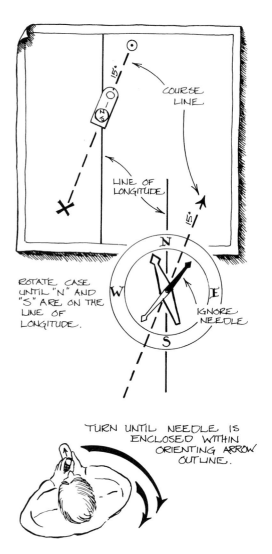

COURSE LINE

LINE OF LONGITUDE

ROTATE CASE UNTIL "N" AND "S" ARE ON THE LINE OF LONGITUDE.

IGNORE NEEDLE

TURN UNTIL NEEDLE IS ENCLOSED WITHIN ORIENTING ARROW OUTLINE.

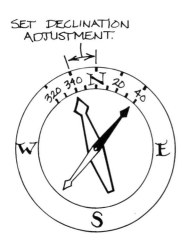

SET DECLINATION ADJUSTMENT.

Map Corrected for Declination

1. Draw lines on the map toward magnetic north.
2. Connect your position and objective with a course line that intersects one of the MN lines.
3. Place the compass's baseplate along the course line and its transparent case over an MN line.
4. Rotate the case until the orienting arrow is parallel to the MN line. For now, ignore the needle.
5. The course is shown where the direction-of-travel line intersects the dial.
6. Hold the compass in front of you and turn your whole body until the needle is enclosed within the orienting arrow's outline. Follow that course.

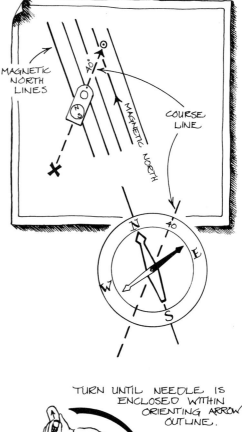

MAGNETIC NORTH LINES

COURSE LINE

MAGNETIC NORTH

TURN UNTIL NEEDLE IS ENCLOSED WITHIN ORIENTING ARROW OUTLINE.

Our trio of pests still invades and obstructs us on all occasions, these are the Musquetoes, eye knats, and prickley pears, equal to any three curses that ever poor Egypt laiboured under.

—Bernard De Voto, editor,
The Journals of Lewis and Clark

LOCATING A MAPPED OBJECT IN THE FIELD

You know where you are, and you see a landmark on the map that might be helpful as a reference point. But when you look up from the map, you're not sure where the landmark is. If it's a mountain peak, it could be clustered with others, making it difficult to spot. What you need is the exact direction from your position to the mark.

To find that direction, draw a line on the map from your position to the known object, determine the direction from you to it, correct for declination, and then aim your compass to that bearing. What it points to is the landmark you selected on the map. As you have probably noticed, this procedure is essentially the same as the one for finding a course.

Compass Corrected for Declination

1. The compass's declination adjustment is set to correspond with geographic north.
2. Mark your position and that of the object. Connect the two with a straight line that extends until it intersects a left- or right-hand border, or a drawn-in line of longitude, which represents geographic north.
3. Place the compass's baseplate along the line toward the object. Slide the compass on this line until its pivot is over a geographic-north line.
4. Rotate the case until north and south on the dial (not the orienting arrow and lines!) are parallel to the geographic-north line. For now, ignore the needle.
5. The bearing to the object is shown where the direction-of-travel line intersects the dial.
6. To locate the object, hold the compass in front of you and turn your whole body until the needle is enclosed within the orienting arrow's outline. Look along the direction-of-travel line to find the object.

40° (MAGNETIC)

Follow the illustrations on page 90 for a declination-adjusted compass. You should see the landmark on the prescribed bearing.

Navigation was a matter of dead reckoning, so many hours at so many miles per hour. The eye was of small assistance. Each esker looked like the last, and each clump of stunted spruce or each rock. Darkness set in shortly after noon. It was not the darkness of night, but rather of a long-extended twilight. The sun not far below the horizon and the extreme whiteness of everything lent fair visibility, but so blurred the outlines of distant knolls as to render them more alike than ever.

—Malcolm Waldron,
Snow Man

Perfect

The most fluid navigational experience I've ever had was on a canoe trip to the Ten Thousand Islands chain in Florida's Everglades National Park. That corner of the park is a maze of mangroves and channels. Knowing *exactly* where you are is critical because all the mangroves do look the same.

While still on the beach in Chockolosky Bay, the outfitter who rented my wife and me our canoe gave us some local beta. We loaded up and shoved off.

Crossing the bay, I realized I had better keep my map and compass out where I could easily refer to them. Laying the map on top of the small cooler we brought and putting the compass on top was perfect—as I paddled, I could see my bearing and stay on it. It was as if the canoe was a bearing needle. I would point to where we wanted to go and that was it—no mountains or canyons in the way.

As we started into the maze of mangroves, I had already become familiar with landmarks, such as they were. Each turn correlated to the map as we paddled across the brackish black water. The channels snaked around and opened into larger waterways, then broke off into a dozen smaller channels. I kept the canoe on my bearings. That evening, which just happened to be Thanksgiving Day, my wife and I ate a turkey breast, stuffing, and cranberries out on a *chickee*, a little platform sitting above the swamp. Just don't ask my wife about the 'gators, because that's a whole other story.

PJC

Map Corrected for Declination

1. Lines are drawn on the map that correspond to magnetic north.
2. Mark your position and that of the object. Connect the two with a straight line that extends until it intersects one of the MN lines.
3. Place the compass's baseplate along the line toward the object. Slide the compass on this line until its transparent case is over a MN line.
4. Rotate the case until the orienting arrow is parallel to the MN line. For now, ignore the needle.
5. The bearing to the object is shown where the direction-of-travel line intersects the dial.
6. To locate the object, hold the compass in front of you and turn your whole body until the needle is enclosed within the orienting arrow's outline. Look along the direction-of-travel line to find the object.

Follow the illustrations on page 89. When you sight along the bearing read from the map, you should see the landmark.

LOCATING AN OBSERVED OBJECT ON THE MAP

In previous procedures, we took a direction from the map and converted it to a compass bearing. Now we'll convert a compass bearing to a direction on the map.

Let's say you see something that would make a good reference point but are not sure where, or if, it is on the map. Because you know your position, a bearing to the object helps locate it on the map. Take the bearing, correct it for declination, and then transfer it to the map, drawing it outward from your position. By looking along the plotted bearing line, you should be able to identify the object.

We did a primitive version of this in chapter 2, sighting the object along a straightedge held over an oriented map. What you will do here is far more accurate and useful. Here's how to proceed.

Compass Corrected for Declination

1. The compass's declination adjustment is set to correspond with geographic north.
2. Take a bearing by pointing the direction-of-travel line at the object and turning the compass case until the orienting arrow aligns with the needle. Read the bearing where the direction-of-travel line intersects the dial.
3. Mark your position. Place a side of the baseplate on your position, with the pivot over a geographic-north line, such as a left- or right-hand border or a drawn-in line of longitude. The direction-of-travel line should be toward the object.
4. Turn the entire compass by the baseplate until north and south on the dial (not the orienting arrow or lines!) are parallel to the geographic-north line. Ignore the needle.
5. Draw a line along the baseplate outward toward the object. You will probably have to extend this line with a ruler for it to cross an object on the map that is similar to the one you see in the field.

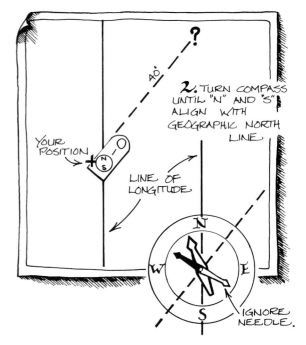

1. TAKE A BEARING.

DECLINATION

2. TURN COMPASS UNTIL "N" AND "S" ALIGN WITH GEOGRAPHIC NORTH LINE

YOUR POSITION

LINE OF LONGITUDE

IGNORE NEEDLE.

Map Corrected for Declination

1. Lines are drawn on the map that correspond to magnetic north.
2. Take a bearing by pointing the direction-of-travel line at the object and turning the case until the orienting arrow aligns with the needle. Read the bearing where the direction-of-travel line intersects the dial.
3. Mark your position. Place a side of the baseplate on your position, with the transparent case over an MN line. The direction-of-travel line should be toward the object.
4. Turn the entire compass by the baseplate (do not rotate the case!) until the orienting arrow is parallel to the MN line. Ignore the needle.
5. Draw a line along the baseplate from your position toward the object. You will probably have to extend this line with a ruler for it to cross an object on the map that is similar to the one you see in the field.

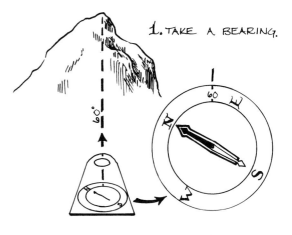

1. TAKE A BEARING.

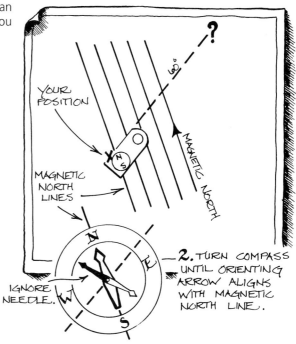

YOUR POSITION

MAGNETIC NORTH LINES

MAGNETIC NORTH

IGNORE NEEDLE.

2. TURN COMPASS UNTIL ORIENTING ARROW ALIGNS WITH MAGNETIC NORTH LINE.

A BEARING FROM A MAPPED OBJECT

Lines of Position

Let's say you can't find your position on the map, but you see a landmark in the distance whose position you can pinpoint.

If you were to take a bearing of the landmark and draw it on the map, you could be sure you'd be *somewhere* on that line. What you have drawn is a line of position—a line of sight upon which you're positioned relative to an object. This may seem to provide little information about your position but, in fact, it eliminates everything except that one line—which is quite a lot. And, as we'll soon see, by crossing one line of position with another, you can find your *exact* location.

Because you don't know your position, you must take a back bearing (described on page 75) to give you the direction from the object toward you. A back bearing is the reciprocal, or opposite, of a normal, or direct, bearing. It's 180 degrees different. Once taken, it is corrected for declination and then drawn from the object on the map.

Compass Corrected for Declination

1. The compass's declination adjustment is set to correspond with geographic north.
2. Take a back bearing by pointing the direction-of-travel line at the object and turning the case until the orienting arrow aligns with the south (not the north!) end of the needle. Read the back bearing where the direction-of-travel line intersects the dial.
3. Place a side of the baseplate on the point that represents the object on the map, with the pivot over a geographic-north line, such as a left- or right-hand border or a drawn-in line of longitude. The direction-of-travel line should be toward where you think you are.

4. Turn the entire compass by the baseplate (do not rotate the case!) until north and south on the dial (not the orienting arrow or lines!) are parallel to the geographic-north line. Ignore the needle.
5. A line drawn along the baseplate toward you from the object is your line of position. You will probably have to extend this line with a ruler.

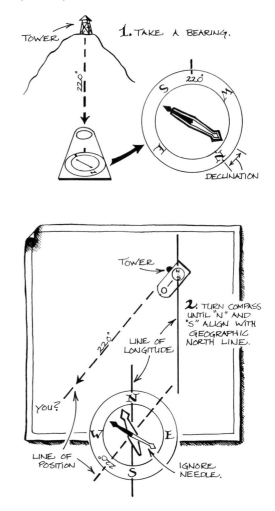

Map Corrected for Declination

1. Lines are drawn on the map that correspond to magnetic north.
2. Take a back bearing by pointing the direction-of-travel line at the object and turning the case until the orienting arrow is aligned with the south (not the north!) end of the needle. Read the back bearing where the direction-of-travel line intersects the dial.
3. Place a side of the baseplate on the point that represents the object on the map, with the transparent case over an MN line. The direction-of-travel line should point toward where you think you are.
4. Turn the entire compass by the baseplate (do not rotate the case!) until the orienting arrow is parallel to the MN line. Ignore the needle.
5. A line drawn along the baseplate toward you from the object is your line of position. You will probably have to extend this line with a ruler.

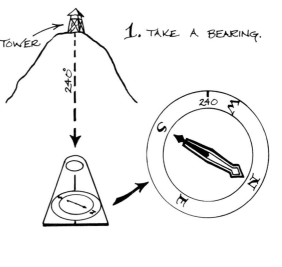

1. TAKE A BEARING.

TOWER

240°

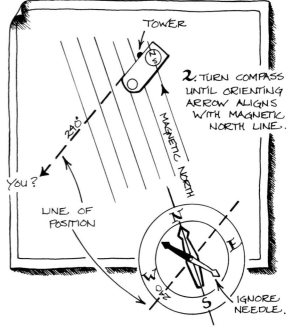

TOWER

2. TURN COMPASS UNTIL ORIENTING ARROW ALIGNS WITH MAGNETIC NORTH LINE.

MAGNETIC NORTH

240°

YOU?

LINE OF POSITION

IGNORE NEEDLE.

OTHER LINES OF POSITION

In the previous section, we used a compass bearing to give us a line of position—a line of sight relative to a known object. But there are other lines of position as well, and for most you don't even need a compass. By studying a map and using a little imagination, you'll see that there are lines of position all around you—you're probably standing on or next to one right now.

The most accurate and easy-to-use lines of position are naturally occurring transits. When two objects in the field line up one behind the other, they form a transit. And a line drawn on the map connecting the two objects makes a perfect line of position with you somewhere on it. A careful look at the map shows a wealth of transits because almost any two mapped and identifiable objects will do. Find them on the map, draw a line through their two points, and extend the line toward your

general area. When you see those two points in the field line up, you are on that line. It's simple and precise.

The "line" in a line of position can be circular as well as straight. If you know how far it is to an object (a skill you'll learn later in this book), you can use that distance as the radius of a circle with the object at its center. You must be somewhere on this circle of position.

Lines of position can also be curved or irregular. Any trail, road, firebreak, ridge, power line, stream, lakeshore, or railroad track is a potential line of position. As long as it's a linear feature that can be found on a map, it qualifies as a line of position.

It's fortunate that there are so many different types of lines of position because, as we'll see on page 100, crossing any two or more of them can give us our exact position on the map. The opportunities are all around us.

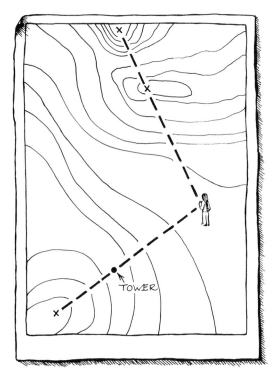

Two transits.

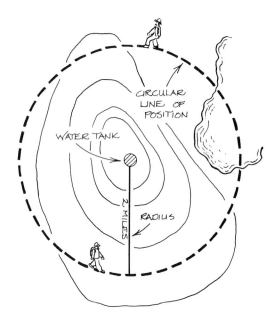

CIRCULAR LINE OF POSITION

WATER TANK

2 MILES

RADIUS

WARNING BEARINGS

Lines of Position for Avoiding Obstacles

Some lines of position, when plotted in advance, can be used to warn of obstacles and keep you out of difficult terrain. A back bearing drawn from a landmark can form one such line of position. Draw a line from a mapped object that lies along your course, skirting the edge of any feature (e.g., a cliff or swamp) that you want to avoid. This line of position is your warning bearing—an invisible barrier over which you don't want to cross.

Draw a second bearing that stands off from the obstacle with a good margin for error; this is the bearing you will walk along. Note the difference between the two bearings and whether the bearings increase or decrease toward the obstacle. This tells

you that you can stray either higher or lower than a particular course and still keep clear. As you travel, continue to check your compass bearing on the landmark until you are sure you have passed the obstruction; this prevents lateral drift from setting you onto it.

Circular lines of position, as described previously, can also be used to keep you away from terrain that you want to avoid. By drawing a circle around such an area, you create an avoidance circle on the map. To keep outside this circle, you need to estimate how far away you are from the object of the circle's center. This technique, adapted from marine navigation, is not often useful to hikers because rolling terrain affords few opportunities for accurate distance estimates—but it's nice to know nevertheless.

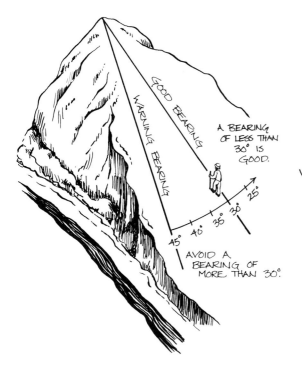

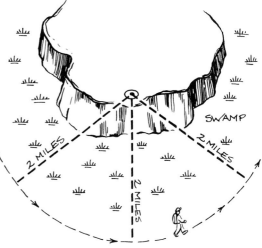

CROSSING LINES OF POSITION

The Fix

While you were napping in the back of Miss Laurel's geometry class, you might have missed this axiom: "Two straight lines can intersect at only one point." It was something to yawn at back then, but it's a perfect definition of what happens when you cross two lines of position. You get a fix—the only spot on the map where you could be.

A single line of position narrows your location to a long, pencil-thin line. But where are you on that line? It's impossible to tell unless you cross it with another line of position. Like two bearings making an intersection in the wilderness, you are at their junction.

Consider the analogy of being lost while trying to find a friend's house. You call her and say, "I'm on Constitution Avenue." That's one line of position. Then you add, "Where it meets 15th Street." Now you've crossed your first line of position with another; you've provided a positive fix. You're one third of a mile south-southeast of the White House in Washington, DC. She'd be able to find you.

In the field, you take back bearings of at least two objects, draw lines on the map outward from their positions, and see where the lines cross. In theory, that's where you are; however, in reality, it is only an approximation. The best bearings most of us are capable of taking are within 1 degree of accuracy, and more often closer to 2 or 3 degrees in error. After a mile, an error like that turns bearing "lines" into a sizable wedge. Therefore, it is safest to consider crossed position lines not so much as a fix as an area of probability.

To reduce this area, lines of position should intersect at 90 degrees, or as close to a right angle as possible. Angles of less than 60 or more than 120 degrees should be avoided. Accuracy can be improved by using nearby objects, and three bearings are always better than two. Indeed, the more bearings the better, assuming all are plotted carefully.

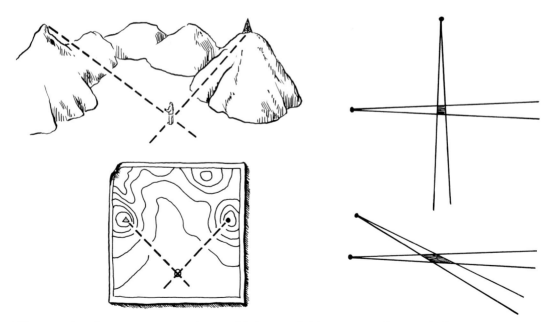

When two bearings cross at an angle near 90 degrees (left), you get a close read of your position (shaded area, upper right). A poor crossing angle (bottom right) yields a sloppy position estimate.

RETURNING TO THE SAME SPOT

A Fix in Reverse

You've found a hidden cave with the Holy Grail in it. Good for you. However, in order to dig it out, you have to go back to town for a shovel and some lunch. Rather than risk losing the treasure again for another few thousand years, you take bearings of at least two landmarks to get a fix—three bearings are better. You could then mark the spot accurately on your map and return to it any time you liked.

But, alas, you do not have a map. All you have is your compass. Well, it's not as bad as you thought. You can still relocate the cave by finding the one spot where those bearings cross.

To return, retrace your steps as best you can until you see one of your landmarks. Then line yourself up on one of the bearings you noted—that is your main highway back. Walk along that bearing toward the landmark until you can take a bearing of the second mark. Continue walking along the first bearing until the second bearing matches what it was originally. When the two (or three) bearings match the ones you originally took, you're back in the same spot. As you'll soon see, this procedure is a variant of the baseline method—particularly when used with a bearing—as described in chapter 5.

This system works for relocating good fishing spots in the middle of a lake or your camp in the middle of nowhere. In unfamiliar terrain, it's a good idea to take a starting fix on your trailhead so that you can find your way back out if plans go awry. The only thing you must do is make a careful note of those landmarks and bearings because you aren't going to remember them.

A RUNNING FIX

There may be times when you want to fix your position but have only one mapped landmark from which to take a bearing. Because a fix is obtained by crossing at least two lines of position, your situation might seem hopeless—unless you know how to take a running fix. This skill requires that you proceed on a straight course and can measure the distance you've covered. The latter is something we'll learn later in this chapter. Meanwhile, here are two useful forms of running fixes.

Two Bearings and a Run

Take a back bearing from an object and plot it on the map. Now walk a straight course until the bearing has changed by at least 30 degrees. Take a second bearing and draw that on the map. Estimate the distance you traveled between the two bearings (see instructions on page 106). Using the map's bar scale, mark the distance on the edge of a piece of paper or measure it with a ruler. Now align your straightedge parallel to your course and spanning the two bearing lines. Slide it out along the bearings (keeping it parallel to your course) until the distance traveled just fits between the bearing lines. The points of intersection indicate your positions at the times you took the two bearings. Use the last one as your fix; it won't be precise, but it will be close.

Doubling the Bearing

This gives you your distance from an object, whether it's on the map or not, by taking two bearings while walking along a straight course. When you take your first

bearing, note how many degrees it differs from your course; this difference is the relative bearing to the object. Hold a straight course and keep taking bearings until you get one that is exactly double the first. If, for example, the first relative bearing was 30 degrees, the second should be 60 degrees. You don't need to plot either of the bearings on the map.

Now estimate the distance you traveled between the two bearings. Through the magic of geometry, that is also the current distance between you and the object. If the object is mapped, you can draw the second bearing on your map, mark on it the known distance from the object—and you have a fix.

The only condition is that the first bearing must be no more than 45 degrees and no less than 10 degrees. Angles of less than 10 degrees introduce a chance for error.

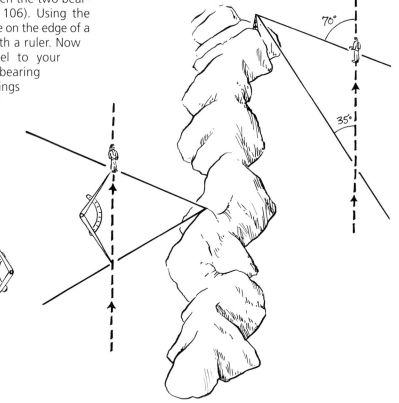

Knowing your distance from something, when you don't know where you are, can put you back on the map. If you are on a line of position (e.g., a bearing, transit, or any linear feature) and can tell how far you are from a mapped object that is also on that line, you can define where you are relative to it.

As we've already seen, finding the distance to (or from) something can also give you a circle of position to help keep you oriented or an avoidance circle to keep you clear of difficult terrain. Then, too, knowing the distance and how long it will take to get to a destination is of great help in planning your day. Distance-off measurements are more often useful to sea kayakers and lake paddlers than to hikers. Nevertheless, these techniques find occasional use on land as well, and are fun to know.

The most accurate way of measuring distance is with a rangefinder, an expensive piece of gadgetry you're not likely to have. In its place we can use some primitive, but surprisingly reliable, techniques.

Estimating Distance by Eye

With some practice, estimating distance by eye can do the job nicely. But the eye can be deceived. Things often appear closer when

- You're looking up or down a hill at them.
- They're brightly illuminated.
- They're seen across water, snow, or flat sand.
- Atmospheric conditions are clear.

  Things often appear farther away when

- The light is poor.
- Their color blends with the background.
- They are over uneven ground.
- Your vision is channeled; for example, down a road or valley.

To estimate distance, use the following as a guide. Try it for yourself when you know how far off things really are. See what they look like, and remember that as a reference.

6 miles: Large houses, small apartment buildings, and towers can be recognized.

2 miles: Chimneys stand out, windows are dots, and vehicles can be seen moving.

1 mile: People look like dots and trunks of large trees can be seen.

½ mile: People look like posts and larger branches on trees become visible.

¼ mile: Head and body forms, leg movement, and colors of clothing become discernible.

250 yards: Faces and hands are blurs but can be seen, as can details on clothing.

100 yards: Eyes appear as dots.

50 yards: Eyes and mouth can be seen clearly.

Finger Angles

Finger angles require you to know an object's height or the width separating two points. You then hold your fingers at arm's length to measure the angle between the object's base and top (for height) or between two points (for width). Enter that angle and the known height or width into the formula to get distance off. Because the height of a particular feature or object is rarely noted on maps, you'll more often use the distance between two points. Look for mountain peaks, two ends of a cliff, two ends of an island, bridge abutments, or any horizontal separation that can be accurately measured on a map.

We shall not cease from exploration
And the end of all our exploring
Will be to arrive where we started
And know the place for the first time.

—T. S. Eliot,
Four Quartets

Distance Off by Winking

You can also measure an angle by winking, using the ten-to-one rule. With one eye closed, hold a finger at arm's length next to one point. Then close that eye and open the other to look at the same finger.

Now estimate to the best of your ability the distance, in miles or yards, that your finger appeared to jump sideways from the first point. Multiply your estimate by ten; that's how far you are from the point—roughly, anyway.

On many occasions, you won't be able to cover a whole length with one wink. But that's all right—try estimating. On a 500-foot-wide island, did your wink get you halfway across or a third of the way?

How Far to the Horizon?

This can come in handy when traveling over open terrain, on larger lakes, or any other place where you have an unobstructed view of the horizon. If you see something sitting just on the edge of the earth's curve (i.e., the horizon) and you know your elevation, you can tell how far off it is. This technique won't work when the terrain between you and the horizon is anything but perfectly flat.

To determine your elevation, look at the map's contour lines. If you're on a boat, by the shore of a lake, or on a flat open plain, you need only know the height of your eye above the flat surface between you and the horizon. The higher up you are,

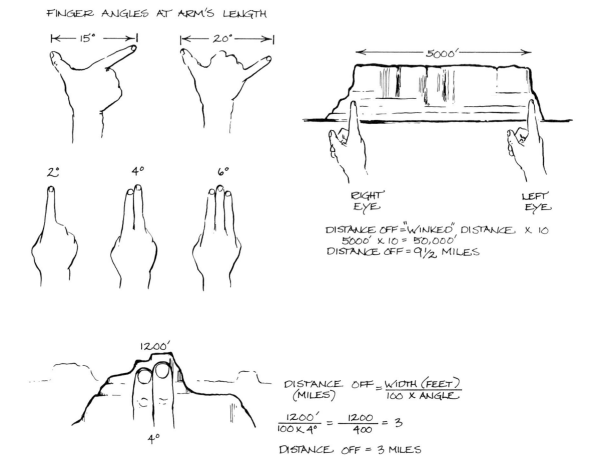

FINGER ANGLES AT ARM'S LENGTH

15° 20°

2° 4° 6°

5000'

RIGHT EYE

LEFT EYE

DISTANCE OFF = "WINKED" DISTANCE × 10
5000' × 10 = 50,000'
DISTANCE OFF = 9½ MILES

1200'

4°

$$\text{DISTANCE OFF (MILES)} = \frac{\text{WIDTH (FEET)}}{100 \times \text{ANGLE}}$$

$$\frac{1200'}{100 \times 4°} = \frac{1200}{400} = 3$$

DISTANCE OFF = 3 MILES

the farther away your horizon is. By taking the square root of your elevation (or height) in feet, you'll find just how far away that is in miles.

This is, in fact, a simplification of a more complex formula, but it's accurate enough. The only hard part is finding the square root; however, because this is only a rough estimation at best, the simplest way to find it is by multiplying a number by itself until you get close to your elevation. A couple of good guesses (or, of course, a calculator) should do it.

If you'll be looking out at the world from a consistent height, as you do when seated in a canoe,

you can measure the height of your eye above the water and accurately figure the square root of it at home. From then on, you'll always know how far it is to the water horizon.

If you want to know how far it is to an object that lies beyond the horizon, you have to allow for the extra distance involved. For example, you see the top of a bold headland long before you see its base, meaning that it is farther away than your horizon. To find out just how far, you have to figure in the headland's height, as well as your own.

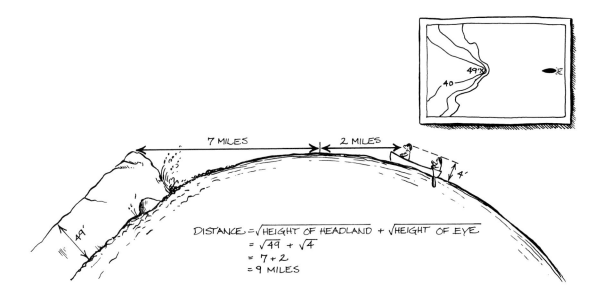

$$\text{DISTANCE} = \sqrt{\text{HEIGHT OF HEADLAND}} + \sqrt{\text{HEIGHT OF EYE}}$$
$$= \sqrt{49} + \sqrt{4}$$
$$= 7 + 2$$
$$= 9 \text{ MILES}$$

MEASURING DISTANCE COVERED

To help plan your journey, you need to know how much ground you can cover within the time available. Once underway, you need even more precise distance information so you can track your progress along a trail, find your position on the map, or estimate how far you still have to go.

Your goal is to accurately measure distance covered. To do this, you can use your stride—the distance you span in a step—which is reasonably consistent and, therefore, useful for measurement. To make things simpler, we'll use your double-stride, the distance covered between every second step, or each time your right (or left) foot comes down; this is usually about 5 feet. To check, walk a measured course of at least 500 feet at your normal pace and stride while counting each time your right (or left) foot touches the ground.

Divide the distance walked by the count to find how far you go with every two steps. This is also a good time to see how many minutes it takes to cover a mile (i.e., 5,280 feet). Armed with this information, you can now measure how far you travel by counting the number of steps you take. If each double-stride is 5 feet, then after 200 steps, you've gone 1,000 feet. Granted, it's a mind-deadening task, but it can be done. Roman soldiers did it; for them, every thousand (or "mille") double-steps became the unit of measure known as a mile. Of course, the stride you measured was under ideal conditions, but it's a good standard that can be modified to suit conditions.

A practical way of counting is to start with a pocketful of pebbles. After each 100 double-strides, shift a pebble to another pocket. To figure the distance covered, count the pebbles and multiply by a hundred. Multiply that amount, in turn, by the length of your stride.

It's about as much fun as filing your taxes, and you wind up with dirt in your pockets. So you may be tempted to buy a pedometer to do the job; don't waste your money—even the new high-tech ones are good only on firm, level ground. As soon as you start climbing over fallen trees, jumping from rock to rock, or scrambling down loose sand, the gadget becomes useless.

It is easier for most people to use time as a measure of distance—easier because our internal rhythm or pulse gives us a natural sense for it. You can probably judge the time of day or how long you've been doing something without looking at a clock. With practice, many of us can come to within 10 minutes of estimating the correct time from the last sunrise or sunset—which is pretty good.

How far can you go in a given time? Back in 1892, W. Naismith, a Scottish mountaineer, came up with the following rule: "An hour for every 3 miles on the map, with an additional hour for every 2,000 feet of ascent."

That works out to 20 minutes per mile on an easy trail with no pack, which is probably only feasible for an athletic hiker on level terrain. Most people can average only 2 miles per hour (i.e., 30 minutes per mile) under good conditions without constant hurrying. With a full pack or on a difficult trail, this can increase to at least 40 minutes per mile; a full pack on a tough trail pushes your time up to 60 minutes. The variables are endless: marshy or rough terrain, thick undergrowth, dense woods, altitude, fatigue, snow or rain, extreme heat or cold, wind, darkness, and pack weight all take their toll. You also lose speed on descents as well as ascents, although only about half as much. And groups of hikers move more slowly than solo hikers.

Use these estimates as a route-planning guide. Study the map, draw slope profiles, or figure out slope gradients. A hike that measures 15 miles on the flat map and ascends 4,000 feet in the real world takes about 9 hours nonstop, and you need at least an extra hour for rest stops. That's a reasonable estimate. You'll find, though, that distances to be covered tend to be underestimated before starting out, and distances traveled are overestimated when walking them. To work out your rate of progress, measure elapsed times and distances covered whenever you can. Write these figures down for later use when all you have is your sense of time and a few pebbles in your pocket.

DEAD RECKONING

There may come a time when landmarks and points of reference are few and far between, or so indistinguishable as to be confusing. It could happen on the plains of Nebraska, Alaska's tundra, or while canoeing a large lake—anyplace where there seems to be nothing with which to work. It could even happen in familiar territory in bad visibility—this situation forces you to stop navigating by eye and begin finding your way by intellect.

The technique used by mariners is called *dead reckoning*—an unfortunate combination of words. But don't be thrown off; the "dead" comes from "ded.," an abbreviation of *deduced*. It's not a reference to a style of navigation practiced on the River Styx; rather, it is position-finding by deduction. You work out where you are relative to a previously known point by using distances and directions traveled from it.

Using Map and Compass

You begin your journey from a positive fix, a point that you are sure of and can locate on the map. From there, you maintain accurate records of distance and direction for each leg of your route.

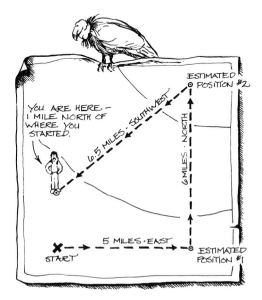

YOU ARE HERE.—
I MILE NORTH OF
WHERE YOU
STARTED.

ESTIMATED
POSITION #2

6.5 MILES · SOUTHWEST

6 MILES · NORTH

5 MILES · EAST

START

ESTIMATED
POSITION #1

You then use these records to update your position on the map.

Here's an example. You want to go for a walk around a ranch with flat terrain. Starting from a spot you can select on the map (say, where a power line crosses a road), choose a compass heading and follow it. Count steps or use some other method to measure the distance you walk. When you decide to change direction, stop. Take out the map and draw a course line out from the starting point in the direction you walked. Measure a distance on that line equal to the distance you traveled. That is where you are now—your dead-reckoning, or DR, position. If you do the same each time you change direction, you'll always know where you are—greatly reducing your chances of becoming buzzard bait.

In theory, dead reckoning works. It also works in reality, but maybe not as well as we'd like. Because it is impossible to walk an absolutely straight compass course, and because our techniques for measuring distance are not inherently precise, DR positions are always a little suspect. This is why any position derived by this method is referred to as an estimated position, which it very well is.

For short distances, such as a few miles, the cumulative errors are acceptable. But going all day without a secure fix is flirting with disorientation. Luckily, though, these times are exceedingly rare unless you're crossing the Greenland ice cap or paddling Lake Superior. Under ordinary circumstances, dead reckoning is merely an interim measure to put you within sight of the next landmark. It's a good way of not getting lost, as long as you accept its limits. Don't be fooled by a cross on a map where your DR position shows you to be. You are more than likely not at that point, just somewhere near it. Dead reckoning does no more than narrow down the area of uncertainty.

Using Compass Only

If necessary, you can find your way home at the end of almost any journey by compass alone. It is always better to work with both map and compass together, but if you find yourself with only a compass, all is not lost.

The key is to divide your outward journey into straight-line legs. Start by following a compass course until you need to turn. At that point, stop and write down the time it took to get there and the direction in which you traveled. Then head off on the new course, noting your new direction and how long it takes to get to the next turning point. Each time you change direction, write down the new course and the time it took to get from the previous turning point. Continue doing this throughout your journey. When you finally decide to head back, you can either retrace your steps or make a beeline directly for home.

Going back the way you came is a simple matter of reading your records in reverse order and converting compass courses to their reciprocals (i.e., 180 degrees different from those you followed on the way out). However, covering the same ground is boring and it's often a longer route home. A better way is to make a straight run back, which is accomplished by converting your records into a "chart," a scaled-down graphic representation of each leg of your trip that is correct for time traveled (distance) and compass courses walked (direction).

This can be done with paper and pencil or with lines drawn in the dirt. Starting anywhere, draw each leg to scale. The end of the last leg represents your current position. From the chart, you can now find the direction back to your starting point, and then follow that direction on the compass. This doesn't give you your position on a map relative to your surroundings, so you really don't know where you are—but that doesn't matter. You do know where you are relative to home and safety—which is just fine.

The main advantage of this system over dead reckoning with a map is that distances are measured in time—not feet, yards, or miles. There's no need for accurate distance measurements, which are hard to make while walking. And there's no need to bother with declination conversions—everything relates to the compass's magnetic north.

This type of dead reckoning was once common on ships at sea, using traverse boards to note courses, distances, and changes in both. Nineteenth-century European explorers in Africa used a similar technique, and Don Paul, a former Green Beret, recently modified it into a complete system of navigation.

All you have to do is record compass courses for each leg and the time spent on them. Then you make a chart from your records. Here's how to make the chart:

1. Find a flat, open piece of ground—the bigger the better.
2. Choose a spot to represent your starting point. Mark it with a stick in the ground.
3. Plot direction for the first leg. From your records, find the compass course you traveled and duplicate that on your chart. If you walked toward 40 degrees, lay the compass on the ground and draw a line in the dirt 40 degrees out from the stick that represents your starting point.
4. Plot distance for the first leg. From your records, find the time it took to walk the first leg. Pick a scale to represent time. The length of your shoe could equal 10 minutes or a hand span could equal 5 minutes. The unit of measurement is unimportant, but consistency is: whatever unit you choose, you must stick with it for the whole chart. Measure out the time traveled along the course line of your first leg, and mark that spot with a stone.
5. Plot the direction and time for all subsequent legs as you did for the first.
6. At the end of the last leg, place a stick in the ground—that is your current position. Lay the compass on the ground and take the bearing of the stick representing your point of departure—that bearing is your direct compass course home.

Unfortunately, this method does not work in mountainous country. Walking times vary too much going up and down steep slopes, thereby making "distances" on your chart inaccurate. It works best where the land is fairly flat.

Refer to time in your notes by the military 24-hour clock system. Remember when subtracting one time from another that there are 60 minutes in an hour, not 100. If you start at 1440 and stop at 1510, you find the difference between the two by subtracting 1440 from 1510, which is 0030 (30 minutes). Be careful; with ordinary numbers, 1,510 minus 1,440 would be 70. Minutes and seconds of time, like minutes and seconds of degrees, are based on the number 60. Incidentally, recording elapsed time is much easier with a stop-watch.

For this kind of dead reckoning to work satisfactorily, you must walk only in straight lines. While you'll find few straight paths in nature, you can break down almost any curve into a series of short straight lines.

Keeping a uniform pace (i.e., walking speed) is important because it affects time. When your speed changes, record it. If you break out of some thick underbrush onto an open field, stop and record it as a new leg, even if your course remains the same.

The bigger the chart, the fewer are the chances of making errors and getting angles wrong. Like map-and-compass dead reckoning, this type is not absolutely precise; however, done carefully, it gets you close. In most cases, that's enough.

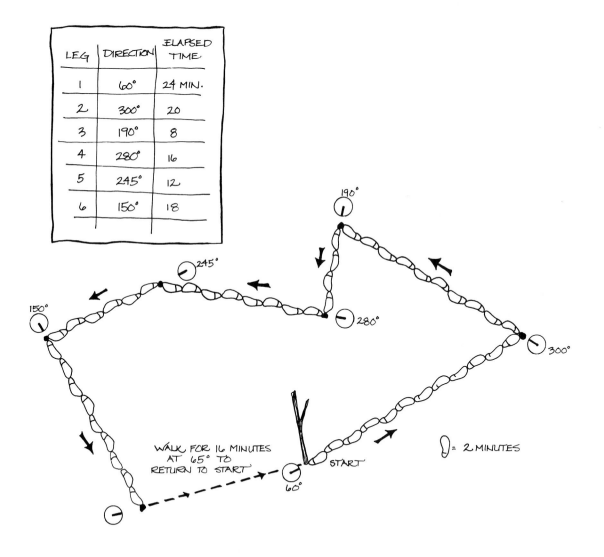

LEG	DIRECTION	ELAPSED TIME
1	60°	24 MIN.
2	300°	20
3	190°	8
4	280°	16
5	245°	12
6	150°	18

190°

245°

150°

280°

300°

WALK FOR 16 MINUTES AT 65° TO RETURN TO START

START

60°

= 2 MINUTES

NAVIGATION IN USE

What you learned in chapter 4 was the mechanics of navigation. While technique is important, it must not be thought of as the culmination of or replacement for the basic tenets of way finding described in the beginning of this book. Don't let the comforting mechanics of using map and compass lull you into complacency. The good navigator needs and employs everything available when out in the field, for there is much more to finding your way than lines on a map or bearings from a compass. As you travel, think of what you and the world around you look like to a bird overhead. Envision the larger picture and your place in it; this is your mental map. Compare it with what you see and what you find on the map in your hands. Do this by continually updating your position through the use of sequential landmarks, or by keeping track of how far and in what directions you have gone. Above all, stay aware of the world through which you are moving. Consider navigation not so much as a technique, but rather as a habit of thought, a practice of awareness of the land and its indicators, and what is going on around you.

At the heart of navigating are three questions: Where am I? Where am I going? How do I get there? Simple questions that require thoughtful answers—answers that can be found with a map, compass, and the ability to discover and decipher clues. Develop all your navigational abilities and trust them, yet remain skeptical and willing to question your judgment. When you can, confirm your observations. Always be sure of where you are, where you are going, and how you will get there.

Let's recap the basic tenets we've learned so far.

- No one has an innate sense of direction. So don't trust yours, trust your compass instead.
- You are not capable of walking in a straight line over long distances without the aid of external clues.
- Most of the directional guides found in nature are unreliable on their own; they need legitimate map-and-compass work to reinforce them.
- A compass and a map cannot get you there or back without skill and effort.
- You can't start navigating when you first feel lost; it must be ongoing from the start.
- When lost, there is no assurance that others will find you. Do what you can to avoid getting lost. If it happens, do what you can to help others find you.

ROUTE PLANNING

Before you head into the wilderness, it's wise to do some pretrip planning. Begin by studying on your map the character of the region you will be traversing and how it affects your choice of routes. Locate your starting point and your objective, then try "walking" an imaginary straight line between the two. It may be the most direct route, but is it the quickest or easiest? Listen to what the map tells you. Note the vegetation, ground surface, and slope gradients. Are the contour lines along your route too close together? Rather than scrambling up and down, would it take less effort to follow a single contour line? It might be a longer journey, but you'd stay at one level. Seek out potential obstacles. A map gives a bird's-eye view of what's around and ahead of you; use it. Choose potential landmarks and good baselines. Plan your route in short segments. Consider the difficulty of the terrain and how far you realistically want to travel. This is also a good time to consider potential campsites.

After selecting a route, use a highlighter to make it stand out from the jumble of other lines. On straight stretches, write the compass courses toward and away (in case you have to backtrack) from your objective, and the distance traveled between course changes. The route you choose now need not be considered final. Things often look different on the trail—you can't know everything from a map—but at least you are heading out with a plan from which intelligent choices can be made.

Use maps to take in the big picture and see beyond the narrow path of your travels. An extra-small-scale map covering a greater area than your large-scale navigational map can be helpful for this. Look for prominent yet distant landmarks to use for bearings. Be aware of main roads and towns, as well as their locations and directions relative to your route. This will come in handy if emergencies occur. You might even find at this point that a map of an adjacent quadrant would be handy. Maps are relatively cheap at the store, but are priceless when they are needed—and unavailable—in the field.

Consider your route back as well. The most straightforward way to return is along the path that takes you in. It may not be as interesting as a different return route, yet it may be necessary if the weather turns. Cover all your options.

Guidebooks and trail guides are an excellent source of information about trails, camps, regulations, and all the nuances a map cannot portray. Check them for their latest revision dates and try to avoid outdated editions. If the guide is too cumbersome to take along, transfer as much information as you can to the map. Note things like shelters, drinking-water sources, trail conditions, and changes made after your map's revision date. Explore other sources of information. Seek out rangers and those whose job it is to know what is going on, but be wary of the ever-present local "expert."

File a travel plan before leaving, giving a written itinerary to a responsible person (see a sample form in the appendix). List the name of every person in your party, the telephone numbers of friends or relatives, where you are leaving your car, what gear you are carrying, where you're headed, your intended route, likely campsites, time of departure, the estimated time and place of your return, and any anticipated side trips. Make sure you provide the names and numbers of authorities to call if you are overdue (e.g., rangers, rescue groups). Finally, make sure that when you return safely, you immediately contact the person with whom you left your travel plan. If you don't, rescuers may unnecessarily risk their lives looking for you.

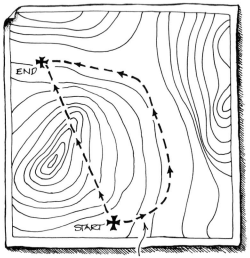

LONGER ROUTE MAY BE EASIER AND FASTER.

THE PRACTICE OF NAVIGATION

Navigation is more state of mind than set procedures. To keep track of your position, you must stay alert and look for opportunities to use a wide variety of techniques. As the land changes, so should your approach to wayfinding.

Effective navigation requires imagination. It draws on all your skills, utilizing the mind as well as the senses. By all means, hone your map-and-compass abilities, but never stray from the rules of basic wayfinding.

When traveling, try to picture your surroundings as if you were looking down from an airplane. Compare this image to what you see around you and what you find on the map. Most important, watch where you are going and practice total awareness of the indicators around you.

That covers the general philosophy of navigation. Now here are some specifics:

Orient the map (align it to the landscape) with your compass before referring to it. The printing may be upside down or at an angle, but it is easier to correlate what you see with what is on the map. This helps you choose the correct fork at a junction or the correct direction on a mountain descent.

Strive to know where you are on the map at all times and the direction in which you are heading. Don't wait until you get an uneasy feeling that you are not 100 percent sure.

Continually update your position through the use of landmarks or by keeping track of how far and in what directions you have traveled. In reality, it is rare to know precisely where you are at every moment. Typically, we leave a known location, pass through areas and intervals of relative uncertainty about our exact whereabouts, and then reestablish an accurate position at every opportunity. This alternating pattern of pinpoint locations and areas of probability continues until we reach our destination.

Restrict the times of ambiguity to a minimum and to keep the areas of uncertainty down to a circle of a few hundred yards (rather than a few miles). Do this by frequently checking your position.

Confirm your position on the map every time you reach a landmark, junction, and fork in the trail, and when you break clear from the woods so you can see the surrounding terrain. Or discipline yourself to stop every twenty minutes to keep a running track of where you might be. Even if you can't ascertain your exact position on these "nav-breaks," you will at least be reducing your area of uncertainty.

Keep a running log (i.e., notes) or a sketch map of your route when bushwhacking or traveling cross-country. This is usually impractical and thus rarely done, but you'll thank yourself for taking this trouble. "Turned to 275 degrees at mouth of pocket canyon. Walked 11 minutes to dry streambed. Followed streambed north for 9 minutes, turned off to 90 degrees facing distant butte. . . ."

Upon leaving major turning points or landmarks, write down next to their position on the map) the time of day. This helps you judge your pace and the distance you're covering. Turn around and look back at every junction, change of direction, and landmark. Study where you came from, the way it looks, and any prominent features. This is what you will see on the return trip. Get to know it now so it will look familiar when you see it again.

Be willing to question your judgment. Keep an open mind and observe objectively, then determine or confirm your position. Do not choose your position on the map first and then make the world conform to it.

Impartially evaluate your judgment by comparing input from a variety of navigational techniques.

Accept that you cannot hold a compass course of better than 4 degrees and that lateral drift may be occurring. By all means, try to prevent it, but make allowance for this possibility when estimating your position.

Use intermediate landmarks when following a compass course, making a number of short legs rather than one long run. This reduces the potential for confusion and disorientation.

Check the map for likely baselines lying across your route. Always aim for a large target and then use it to lead you toward your objective. Utilize the practice of aiming to one side of your destination. More details are given in this chapter under the heading "Aiming Off."

Think of navigating toward an objective as constantly narrowing down areas of possibility. Use coarse navigation to get you into the general vicinity, then ever-increasing precision to search out your goal. It's like driving in a city you don't know. You take an interstate to the city, then a main avenue to the neighborhood, locate the right street, and then find the block and house. Each choice gets you closer to your destination.

Study the map for a prominent feature near your destination, something that can be easily reached, located, and identified. Head toward that first, then start your precision navigation from there.

Choose landmarks that will not be obscured or, if they are, only intermittently. Try to keep your goal and starting point in sight. Barring that ideal situation, keep at least one landmark in sight at all times.

Maintain a point or line of reference. Ideally, this is something that is always visible, such as a ridge. If not, use something whose existence is confirmed by the map—for example, a road running parallel to your route but a quarter-mile away. Locate yourself and your route in terms of direction toward and distance from this reference.

Don't feel you must use every landmark. Just keep track of the more obvious features beyond your immediate route, while concentrating on the finer details along your path.

As much as possible, stick to your chosen route. This way, even if you can't find your destination, you'll be able to retrace your steps.

Never depend on your sense of direction, a "feeling," or a hunch. Base all decisions on facts. Be opportunistic. Make use of all your observational and navigational skills.

Hold the Pepperoni

When I was a young man, I did my duty to country and enlisted in the Air Force, and it proved to be a great way to work my way through college. One thing I didn't expect, though, was an education in navigation. I was assigned to a medical unit, which each year was sent out into the field, away from the warmth and security of our clinics and waiting rooms, to hone our skills. There were all kinds of green canvas tents, lectures on field procedures, obstacle courses with stretchers, those always-appetizing MREs (military parlance for "meals ready to eat"), and "scenarios"—

imaginary medical emergencies dreamed up by our superiors to test our skills.

One night, the lectures had gone well past dark and into dinner. As the instructor was wrapping up, several of the other instructors came in and dropped a scenario on the group of roughly 30 people—some kind of nighttime triage rescue with full chemical warfare gear. After the usual organizational stuff, I found myself in one of six groups of medics wandering around the dark woods in a hot plastic suit, trying to follow map coordinates given to us by our instructors.

As we hauled around our stretcher-bound "victim" by flashlight, it was difficult to stay on bearing in the woods. We could see the other groups wandering around the woods as well. The route led through an obstacle course, down a ravine, and up a nasty hillside. When we finally topped out on the hill, there was a tent set up to serve as a field hospital. When we entered with our patient, we were greeted with a pizza party to reward us for sound navigation. The other groups —still wandering around—missed the good stuff.

PJC

You wouldn't think there is a need for navigation on a trail. But, you start walking—expecting something like a freeway with well-marked exits—and, well, somehow you blunder off into trouble.

As you may have noticed, trails have little in common with highways, which is why more people get lost on trails than you'd expect. Every exit on a highway is an opportunity to pinpoint your position; every intersection on a poorly marked trail is a chance to make the wrong choice without realizing it.

Even on a well-worn trail, it makes sense to know where you are. Usually the only compass work you need to do is when you're orienting the map. From then on, it becomes a matter of keeping track of consecutive landmarks, relating your movement to references, and remembering distances and directions traveled. Try to maintain a running record in your mind of the path you followed. If the route has been circuitous, keep a written log or make a simple sketch map. Both are good for finding your position and a route back.

Trails offer the easiest path from A to B. You'll definitely stand a better chance of not getting misplaced by following a trail, straying from it only when you are absolutely sure you know where you are on the map, and when you have a planned route to your destination. Be aware, however, that in many wilderness areas, you are requested to stay on trails for ecological reasons.

Incidentally, don't give up a trail until it either disappears or heads off in a direction that is obviously wrong. When confronted with a situation like this, confirm your position on the map, head back to the last fork or junction, and replan your route. Do not set off blindly, bushwhacking in what you assume to be the right direction. There's usually a very good reason why there are no trails where you are headed.

Unfortunately, trails may foster unwarranted confidence. Don't be too sure that you won't get disoriented when you leave the trail or that you'll be able to return to it, no matter what. A trail is just a thin scrape on the land, and it's not that easy to identify once you're separated from it. You may say to yourself, "I'm only going to take a brief shortcut, why bother with the map or compass?" Trails have a strange way of disappearing.

Watch out for poorly maintained, old, or marginal-looking trail markers—they could mean you're on a trail to nowhere. It's even possible that they were made by wildlife, and you might not be interested in good forage. Cairns are often built by people who were lost. Markers may also be missing or destroyed; be suspicious—be even more suspicious when there are no markers at all.

Maps, too, can be disappointing. Many of the clearly marked trails on your park map—the ones that look so obvious and easy to follow—may in reality be poorly maintained, overgrown, or rudimentary in the first place. In large parks or national forests, there may be too many trails for mapmakers to inspect and keep current.

Keep track of where you are so as not to lose your feeling for directions. If your visibility is suddenly limited by thick woods, fog, rain, darkness, or snow and the trail "disappears," where do you go? The same can happen on rough terrain, where we tend to watch only where we are stepping—directly ahead of us. This makes it easy to miss a turn or go off on an unmarked path. As in all navigation, when on the trail, watch where you are going.

CAIRN · PAINT · METAL BADGE · SIGNS · BLAZE

Trail markers. Know what they mean, but please refrain from making your own—you might confuse future hikers.

HITTING WHAT YOU AIM FOR

Baselines

Bushwhacking through thickets, traversing sharp inclines, and weaving around trees all test the limits of your ability to hold a precise course. Your compass may be the best there is, and you may use it with great skill, but you could still wind up between 4 and 8 degrees off course after a long trek. In addition to the terrain, factors working against you include the fact that most compasses can't be read to less than 1 degree, deviation may have gone unnoticed, lateral drift occurred, your sighting technique may be a little sloppy, or an old map may have given you an outdated declination, which you, in turn, made errors in applying. Each throws you off by a small amount, but the cumulative error can be substantial.

To offset these limitations, aim for something big. Optimism is laudable, but do not believe that you will always be able to hit what you aim for. Put the odds in your favor by leaving room for error.

One solution is to choose destinations on a *baseline*. This is a long reference line running across your intended course, making it a hard target to miss. A baseline can be as real as a road, stream, coastline, fence, railroad tracks, power line, ridge, or the steep side of a valley. It can also be an imaginary line—a bearing from a compass.

A map helps you locate the baselines around you or take note of them as you travel. One of the most commonly used baselines is the road where you leave your car at the trailhead. With a good baseline, you don't even need to keep track of your exact course. If you know the general direction of the baseline, and it's long enough, you can always find it. For example, if you parked your car on a north–south road, you could wander in a generally westward direction and know that all you had to do was head vaguely eastward to hit the road again—no straight courses to follow and a minimum of compass work. The only problem is this: when you get to the baseline, which way is your destination?

Aiming Off

Given that you will make mistakes and not be able to hold a precisely accurate course, let your mistakes work for you. Make them purposeful, big, and so far to one side that they are no longer mistakes but rather deliberate offsets.

If you try to hit your target dead-on, but can't find it when you arrive at the baseline, you won't know whether to turn to the right or the left. But if you make sure that you are a long way off to one side, there won't be any mystery. You will know without doubt which way to turn. *Aiming off*, as it is known, is an important technique.

How far off course should you aim to be? Well, the average course error is about 3 degrees, so aiming off by 5 degrees to one side of the direct course to the destination should do it. Always trend toward one side while you're traveling. When you encounter a tree or a rock, go around it toward the side you are aiming for. This way, you always drift off to the same side.

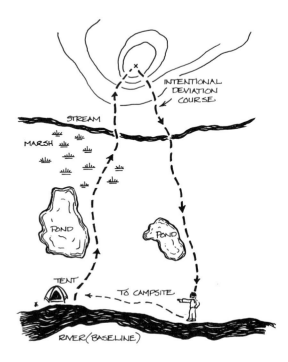

Bracketing

Figuratively, *bracketing* encloses your destination by establishing landmarks on either side of it along the baseline. Navigators use this technique as a backup to aiming off.

If you find the baseline close to your destination and for some reason head off in the wrong direction, you will soon come across a "bracket" telling you to turn back; your destination is the other way.

Brackets can be existing features—there should be no need to make marks or place flags. They must be far enough apart to encompass even the broadest amount of lateral drift. For example, if you are using a river for a baseline, your brackets could be a dam, rapids, falls, bridge, cove, or where a tributary joins. If you have one bracket upstream of your goal and another downstream, you are well bracketed and will know which way to turn if and when one is encountered.

If no obvious brackets show up on a map, walk the baseline in each direction. You may find landmarks not shown on the map. Keep notes on which brackets are where. Then, when you're coming back tired and not thinking clearly, you won't have to guess on which side the burned tree or the huge boulder was. Within the two outer brackets, there can be any number of secondary brackets. Record these, too, with a note something like, "Jeep on road. Abandoned shack ¾ mile to north. Lightning-scarred oak to south, ½ mile out. Small pond touches road 1 mile out."

Bracketing not only tells you in which direction to turn once you reach the line, but also that the line you've reached is the right one. For instance, in areas laced with logging roads, you know you've hit the right one when you see your brackets. This is particularly helpful to hunters or collectors, who randomly explore an area and do not keep a precise track of their route.

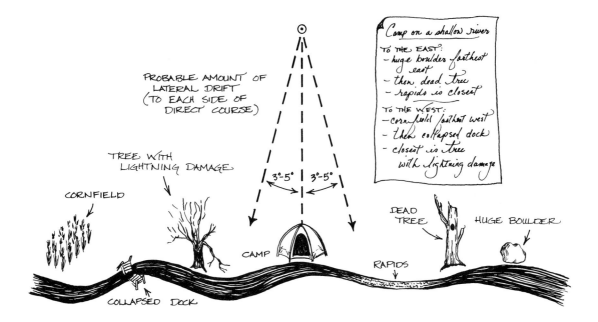

A Bearing as a Baseline

A baseline need not be tangible. It can just as well be an abstract creation such as a compass bearing. Where there are few landmarks, or where they are inconveniently placed, a bearing used as a baseline may be your savior.

Suppose you are leaving your campsite in the morning and want to be sure you can find it in the afternoon. Take a bearing from your starting point toward a prominent landmark. Write that bearing down; it is now your baseline. Go out and wander around. When you want to return, line yourself up with the landmark so you are on the baseline bearing. Assuming you aimed off toward the landmark, the reciprocal—or back bearing—is your route home.

This technique isn't limited to a return to your own starting point. Anytime a prominent mapped

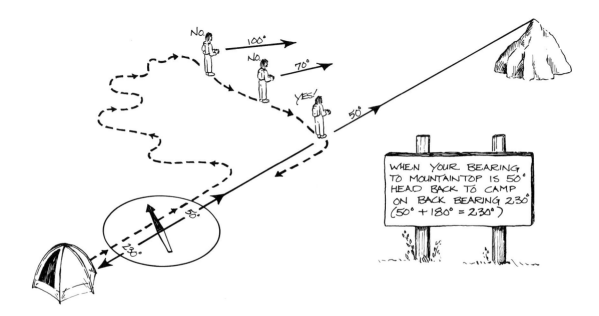

landmark—say, a peak dominating a valley—will be visible from your destination, you can take its bearing from the map and use that as a baseline.

A bearing of one landmark gives you a baseline. Add a second bearing of another landmark, and you can tell where you are on that baseline. This is the principle of crossed bearings, which asserts that there is only one spot where two bearings can cross.

In practice, you walk until you are on one bearing, which becomes your baseline. You then take a bearing of the second landmark to determine which direction you should walk on the baseline to make this second bearing match what it should be at your destination. This is the same technique described previously about how to return to a position established from two bearings (see page 101).

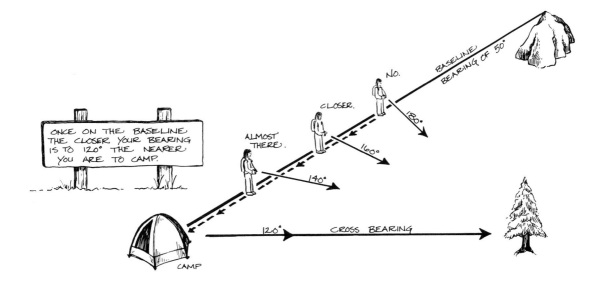

ONCE ON THE BASELINE THE CLOSER YOUR BEARING IS TO 120° THE NEARER YOU ARE TO CAMP.

ALMOST THERE.

CLOSER.

NO.

BASELINE BEARING OF 50°

180°

160°

140°

120°   CROSS BEARING

CAMP

LANDMARKS AS GUIDES

Handrails and Catch Points

Some landmarks are valuable because they enable you to navigate without a compass, and sometimes even without a map. Let's have a look at the features called *handrails* and *catch points*.

Handrails

These are long, natural or man-made features running parallel to your course. They're called *handrails* because you symbolically latch onto them and follow where they go. The handrail becomes your guide.

A typical handrail is a fence, a road, the edge of a field, a ridge, a valley, a lake- shore, power lines, or a stream. There's no need to be in actual contact with it; as long as you can maintain a parallel course, the handrail is doing its job.

You can also think of a handrail as a highway. When you find one, you can put your map and compass away for a while and cruise along as if you were on an interstate.

Catch Points

Look on the map for an easily identifiable landmark that shows where to leave the handrail (or highway) and turn onto a new course. These indicators, called *catch points* or sometimes *collecting features*, tell you it's time to leave the handrail highway. They also confirm your position on the handrail, which—when reached—should be checked on the map.

Almost any mapped feature can be a catch point. And catch points aren't always points either; they can be lines, such as a trail crossing your course—which could be used as another handrail. The number of possible handrails and catch points is vast. Look for them; use them.

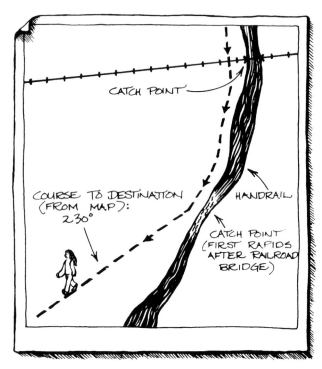

CATCH POINT

COURSE TO DESTINATION (FROM MAP): 230°

HANDRAIL

CATCH POINT (FIRST RAPIDS AFTER RAILROAD BRIDGE)

SOURCES OF ERROR

We all make mistakes; we simply have to accept that fact. The best we can do is be aware and catch them before they do too much damage. Our instruments make mistakes, too, which can induce us to make even greater mistakes of our own. Here are some common errors we're all likely to commit at one time or another.

Map Errors

- Using an old map that has not been recently updated.
- Using privately made and printed maps that do not adhere to National Map Accuracy Standards. If they do, it says so on the map.
- Mistaking the plus symbol (+) where lines of latitude and longitude cross for the X symbol (bench mark), and not understanding why you can't locate the bench mark.
- Drawing MN lines to the angle of the MN arrow on the declination diagram rather than to the actual declination angle printed next to it.
- Not accounting for annual changes in declination.
- Using directions from a map directly on a compass without adjusting for declination.
- Using a distance-measuring scale on the side of a baseplate compass that does not match the map's scale.
- Inaccurately transferring distance from the bar scale to the map.
- Using a map with a scale too small to show helpful details or give accurate bearings.
- Reading the protractor incorrectly when choosing a direction.
- Failing to correlate the map correctly with your surroundings.

Compass Errors

- Using the north end of the needle to give a bearing instead of the direction-of-travel line or arrow.
- Confusing the north and south ends of the needle. North is usually painted red.
- Overestimating a compass's limits of accuracy (usually between 2 and 4 degrees).
- Not taking careful bearings. Always use the same eye when sighting along a compass, and take bearings twice to be sure.
- Overlooking sources of deviation. Compasses are affected by nearby magnetic objects such as radios, knives, belt buckles (even those that look like brass), cameras, battery-powered watches, guns, overhead power lines, and railroad tracks. Never place a compass on the hood of a car to do map work.
- Taking directions with a compass and plotting them directly on a map without compensating for declination.
- Using a compass in a magnetic zone other than the one for which it was intended.

General Navigation Errors

- Calculating incorrectly when correcting for declination.
- Applying declination in the wrong direction.
- Not recording courses and distances with care and in a manner that will be easily understood.
- Not making many short legs of a long course and not using intermediate landmarks.
- Ignoring the possibility of lateral drift.
- Accepting "local knowledge" without reservation.

WHEN YOU ARE LOST

The day may come when you lose a trail, can't decide which way to go at a junction, or see something that doesn't look right. If you can follow your route back, you are not lost. But if you continue, you could, within an hour or so, very easily become completely lost. This is why you must keep constant track of your position and never charge ahead blindly with hope in your heart (and map and compass buried in your pack).

As soon as you get that slight twinge of uncertainty, stop to get out your map and compass. Retrace your steps in your mind and on the map. Find that last point where you were absolutely positive about your position, and use that as a reference. With the map oriented, look carefully for landmarks and clues around you. If you are becoming nervous or too worried to think clearly, make this nav-break into a rest stop. At this point, the worst that can happen is that you have to walk back the way you came until you are sure of where you are, and then proceed once again from there.

But what happens if you are truly lost? Let's presume you've unknowingly been misreading landmarks and walking the wrong trail for hours without seeing anything wrong. Then the trail stops where it shouldn't. You have convinced yourself all day that what you saw made sense. Now it doesn't—and now you're lost, good and proper.

The first thing to do is stop and admit that you don't know where you are. Don't blunder onward, letting your pride and "sense of direction" take over. Confess your sins so you can begin to undo them.

Fear—with the disbelief, frustration, and panic that accompany it—is the most debilitating result of getting lost. Once it takes hold, you lose your ability to think clearly, see what's around you, and reason objectively. The best way to prevent this is to stop panic before it starts. To calm yourself, remember that at an average speed of perhaps 2 miles per hour, you can't have strayed too far from the rest of the world. So take off your pack, have a snack, and relax for a while. Sort things out calmly. Let other members in the group know what's going on, build confidence, and start looking for clues. Most of the time, you can reconstruct your mistakes and figure out how you got to where you are and, from there, how to get back. If not, you'll soon be found by others. (You did leave a travel plan with someone, didn't you? No? Well, maybe it won't be so soon, after all.) Records show that most lost hikers are found within two or three days.

Orient the map, ask everyone to recall details of landmarks passed, look for prominent features, use all your senses, and try to piece things together. Do not give in to wishful thinking by hastily identifying what you see and making it fit what you want to see. Be cool, be objective. Think of being lost as starting a jigsaw puzzle; begin by gathering the pieces that make up the border, and work inward. From all your data, draw a circle of possibility on the map, a broad area within which you think you're located. That's the border to your puzzle. It's just an estimate, but it's a start and will help direct your thinking. It also breeds confidence—at least now you're on the map.

Look beyond your circle of possibility for hard-to-miss baselines. A river, highway, lake—anything that makes a giant target you can't miss. In case you can't find exactly where you are, so as to be able to continue your hike, the baseline gives you a way back to help. Just head in its general direction until you hit it. You may not be sure where you are on the baseline, but you have now established a valuable line of position that will soon yield more clues and give you a fix.

By the way, there is an old chestnut of backwoods lore that says: "If you follow a river downstream, it will lead to civilization." Don't believe it. No matter which way you turn, your chances are even.

When nothing seems to be coming together, it's time to start scouting about or retracing your steps—searching the immediate area for trails, markers, or anything that can help; however, don't get more lost than you are. You followed some logical route (at least, it seemed so at the time) to get where you are, so there is a chance of finding your way back. But if you start wandering aimlessly about, you may lose even this thin thread of connection. You may become not just simply lost, but profoundly lost—and there is a difference.

Look around you, note carefully what you see, and take bearings on landmarks or put a stick in the ground. This is home base. However, even though it's home, take your pack with you when you leave to go exploring. Imagine how stupid you'd feel if you left your pack behind and couldn't find it again. From now on, everyone stays tightly together. You don't want to risk becoming separated. First, head for high ground or climb a tree for a better view. Follow a compass course out from home base so you can find your way back. Nothing? OK, then go back to home base.

Next, start making short, straight-line reconnaissance runs out and back to all the cardinal and intercardinal points. If that turns up nothing, then it's time to start a search pattern.

Take out pencil and paper. From home base, head in any cardinal direction (write it down). Walk for a mile, or about 30 minutes (write that down, too). Stop, turn 90 degrees, and begin walking 1-mile legs (and recording all this, along with landmarks passed) until you make a complete square that brings you back to home base. You will have covered a square mile. If you find nothing, make more 1-mile squares by heading out in the remaining three cardinal directions to give you a thoroughly

covered 4 square miles. In an area as large as that, you're bound to find something that you can positively identify on your map.

A word of caution: forget about any of these scouting activities if dusk is descending. Being lost in the dark is about as bad as it gets—until, that is, a storm hits as well. So pitch camp, get settled, make a fire, and start organizing a plan of action for tomorrow. Consider how you will find your way out or how you can help others find their way in to you.

This last option, staying put and signaling for help, may become a realistic one if you simply can't get a grip on the situation. You can help searchers by staying out in the open or on high ground. You can build a smoky fire (don't burn down the forest in the process) and make noise with a whistle. Yelling doesn't carry far and ruins your voice so you can't properly thank your rescuers. And you can lay out distress signals on the ground. Don't move about; stay in one place and let them know where it is. Make yourself conspicuous, even if it means wearing plaids and stripes together. With any luck, it won't come to that.

WALK A "SQUARE SPIRAL" UNTIL YOU FIND A LANDMARK.

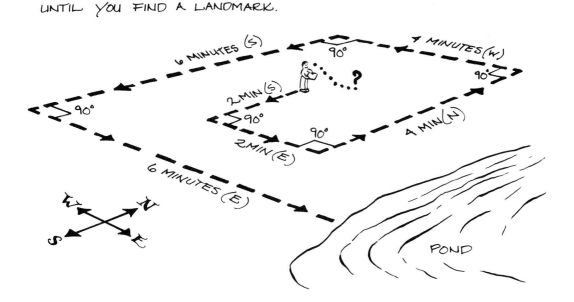

6

LOOKING TO NATURE FOR CLUES

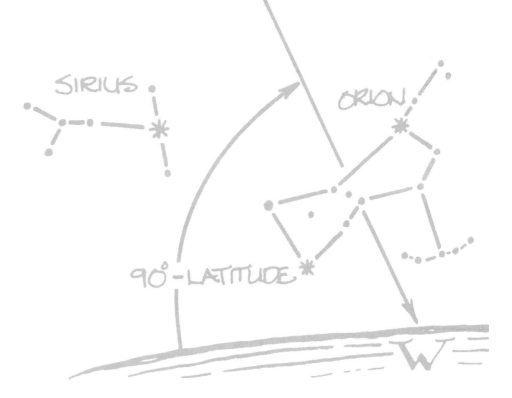

When looking to nature for clues about direction, look to the sky first. What you find at ground level isn't going to help nearly as much or as consistently.

Most of what we hear about "nature's guideposts" is either misleading or just plain wrong. The best example is that old saying about moss growing on the northern side of trees in the Northern Hemisphere. Go for a walk in the Pacific Northwest or in any dense, damp forest. You'll see moss on the north, all right—and some on the south, some on the north *and* south, and some on all sides. The "logic" behind this bit of folklore is that the northern side gets less (or no) sunlight, so the moss flourishes. In reality, what is more important to moss or lichens is moist surroundings, which can be affected by the wind as well as the sun. Therefore, the prevailing winds, local weather, and even the surrounding landscape determine where you find moss.

Here are some other well-known items of wayfinding lore of which to be wary:

Snow in the Northern Hemisphere tends to be finer and less granular on the northern side of a hill, mountain, or ridge. (In practice, such distinctions are fuzzy at best, and often overwhelmed by effects of local terrain and microclimate.)

Snow melts slower on north-facing slopes in the Northern Hemisphere. (This one is often true.)

The branches of most trees in the world's temperate regions grow better and are bushier on the side facing the noon sun—although common spruce, firs, and cedars are not affected in this way. (There are too many other factors at work for this to be reliable.)

Almost all trees that stand in the open have thicker annual rings on their northern sides (Northern Hemisphere), with the heart of the tree closest to the south. (Growth rings are completely unreliable because variable width is the normal response to innumerable stress factors.)

Southern slopes have more and thicker vegetation than northern slopes. (This is possible for steep slopes in extreme high-latitude climates.)

Anthills north of the equator are on the southern side of objects. (This is unverified, to the best of our knowledge.)

Sunflowers are supposed to face the noon sun. (Observations suggest that they more often face the rising sun; besides, how often are sunflowers at hand?)

Paint first fades and peels on the side that gets the most sun. (Strong prevailing winds from another direction would put the lie to this—anyway, if you're looking at a house, you're probably not lost.)

Now we return to camp. While eating supper, we very naturally speak of better fare, as musty bread and spoiled bacon are not palatable. Soon I see Hawkins down by the boat, taking up the sextant—rather a strange proceeding for him—and I question him concerning it. He replies that he is trying to find the latitude and longitude of the nearest pie.

—John Wesley Powell,
The Exploration of the Colorado River and Its Canyons

Similarly, all over the world there are specific plants reputed to be able to point out directions. Here in the United States, from Ohio to the Rockies and Texas to Minnesota, you can find the pilot weed (*Silphium lacinatum*). It grows to about 4 feet and mostly holds its leaves in a north–south alignment when it's in sunlight. Often called the compass of the prairies, it gets honorable mention in Longfellow's "Evangeline."

"Look at this vigorous plant that lifts its head from the meadow,

"See how its leaves are turned to the north, as true as the magnet; . . . "

He's right, but old Henry was obviously no navigator. All of nature's direction-pointing is done relative to geographic, not magnetic, north.

Another well-known plant, one that grows in the American Southwest and Central America, is the giant barrel cactus (*Ferocactus acanthodes*). It grows faster on the shady side than on the sunny side, which almost always makes it lean toward the south. And there are others; file them away as part of your "awareness quotient," such as that game trails often lead to water and that swales showing signs of carrying water during storms should lead to brooks, which should lead to feeder streams, which should lead ultimately to the stream or river that drains the local watershed. Careful reading of the topo map tells you roughly where the watershed limits are.

It doesn't hurt to know that gulls and other shorebirds seen winging overhead at dusk are probably returning to rookeries on the shore or a near-shore island, or to know how the local vegetation changes with elevation. (The Southwest sequence of saguaro and mesquite yielding to juniper and pinyon, then to oak and ponderosa pine, then to Douglas fir and aspen, and finally to spruce and fir with increasing altitude is a dramatic example.) Such knowledge brings its own reward of connectedness to the landscape around you. However, use such indicators only as rough guides, looking for confir-

mation from other sources whenever you can. Signs in the heavens are always dependable—so look up.

In this chapter, we work with the five stars easiest to find. In the Northern Hemisphere, there's Polaris; in the Southern Hemisphere, we use the Southern Cross. East and west are found with the help of Orion in the winter and Scorpio in the summer. That takes care of your nighttime navigation, which—for the sake of safety—should be limited until you've built up experience.

At daylight, you have a fifth star with which to work: the sun. And, as you'll see, a lot of information can be deduced from it during the course of a day. If you can approximate its path, you have a perfect reference line from dawn to dusk.

When the stars are your only source of direction, choose your routes carefully and look for other signs along the way.

There are many ways to navigate without a map or compass, but I habitually use only two—the sun and the wind, and then only as backups. Knowing where they should be in relation to my route means I am quick to notice if their position has shifted. If I've veered off my intended line of travel—easy to do in rolling grasslands or continuous forest—I stop and check my location. I also check that the wind itself hasn't shifted, and what the time is so that I know where the sun should be.

—Chris Townsend,
The Backpacker's Handbook

FINDING NORTH AND SOUTH AT NOON

Halfway through its daily journey from sunrise to sunset, the sun is directly to your south (or north in the Southern Hemisphere). This may not be true in the tropics, between latitudes 23 ½ degrees north and 23 ½ degrees south. There, the sun is almost directly overhead. And it may not be true in the polar regions, where the sun doesn't set or doesn't rise for months at a time. Everywhere else, though, the sun provides a good indicator of north and south.

The trick is knowing when the sun has reached its halfway point, or noon. The "sun's noon," when shadows run north and south, rarely coincides with the noon on your watch. "Watch noon" is affected by factors such as daylight saving time and where you are within your *time zone*, a band of longitude 15 degrees wide in which every timepiece is set to a common noon. This is done to reduce chaos, because for every degree of longitude you travel east, the sun's noon occurs 4 minutes earlier.

Without time zones, someone to the west of center would take their noon lunch break later than someone to the east of center. Then, too, the earth's slightly irregular rotation causes watch time, or average time, to differ from the sun's time by as much as 16 minutes. So you may as well forget about using your watch to time the sun's noon.

What you can do instead is use your watch to measure the length of day from sunup to sundown, and then divide that in half to find midday, the sun's noon. Using 24-hour notation, record the time of sunrise and sunset, subtract sunrise from sunset to get the length of day, divide this by two, and add that to the time of sunrise to get noon.

For example, let's say today the upper rim of the sun came into view at 0720 and disappeared below the horizon again at 1738. Subtracting 0720 from 1738 yields 1018—that's the length of time the sun spent above the horizon. Dividing that by two yields 0509, half a day. Adding 0509 to 0720 yields 1229, your local noon.

You now know that at 1229 the sun will throw a shadow that runs north and south (that's geographic, not magnetic, north). This system works as long as your watch keeps steady time; it even works if your watch is set for another time zone. As long as the period between sunrise and sunset is measured accurately, you'll be fine.

One drawback to this system is that if you time sunrise first and then sunset, noon has already passed. Luckily, though, the sun changes its course through the heavens so slowly that you don't need to take the time of sunrise and sunset on the same day. You could record sunset as you make camp and then sunrise the next morning at breakfast. This way, you know when to expect noon later that day to check your north–south bearing at lunch.

Of course, where the horizon is obscured by the terrain, you won't be able to time the sunrise and sunset accurately. You'd do well to note these times from the daily almanac of a local newspaper before you head off onto the trail.

This same system works equally well with a full moon. If the full moon is bright enough to throw a shadow, you have a good north–south indicator around "lunar midnight," when the moon is halfway across the sky. Furthermore, if you know that the local sun's noon is at 1230, then you also know the full moon bears due south at 30 minutes past midnight. This is so because, by definition, the full moon is exactly on the opposite side of the earth from the sun. Warning: it's tough to tell a "full" moon within four days unless you know the date from a calendar or almanac.

NORTH AND SOUTH FROM A SHADOW

What if your watch has stopped? There is a way of finding where the sun's noon shadow will lie when you have only a rough idea of when midday will occur.

The sun travels a uniform arc through the sky, with noon as its midpoint. Whatever its height is at a given time before noon, it will be at an equal height the same length of time after noon. The sun's height is reflected in the shadows it casts: the longest shadows are formed at sunrise and sunset, the shortest at noon. A morning shadow slowly shortens as midday approaches, and then begins to lengthen as noon passes. If you measure that shadow's length in the morning, it eventually returns to the same length sometime in the afternoon. When it does, the sun has traveled an equal distance each side of noon—which is how we find the midday shadow and, from that, north and south.

To do this, you need a vertical object—a flag-pole, ski pole, walking stick, or even a pencil will do, although shadows from taller objects are easier to measure. By some means (most likely with a weight dangling from a string), you must be sure

that the object is plumbed absolutely vertical on a patch of smooth, horizontal ground. Make your first measurement with a piece of string or a stick, and mark the end of the shadow with a stone. Do this when you are sure it is before the sun's noon, yet as close to it as possible (so you won't have long to wait for the next measurement).

Now sit back and watch as the shadow gets smaller and then longer again, all the while changing its direction. Once it has returned to its original length, mark the shadow's end. Connect the two marks with a straight line, and find its middle—that's where the shadow was at noon. A line from the vertical object to the midpoint of the connecting line runs north and south.

This system works almost everywhere, regardless of your latitude or the time of year. The only drawbacks are that you have to wait what could be hours during the middle of the day. Then, too, at certain times of the year near the polar circles, the sun's shadows are so long as to be impractical to measure. And in areas near the equator, shadows are often impractically short or else they change imperceptibly, making them difficult to measure. Almost everywhere else, however, this is a reliable way to find north and south.

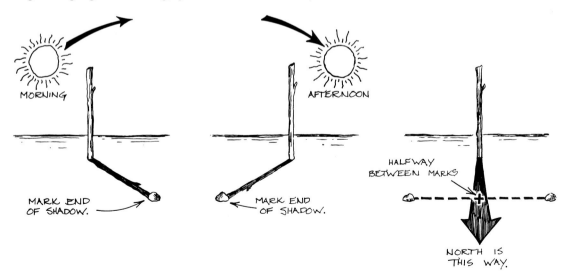

MORNING

AFTERNOON

MARK END OF SHADOW.

MARK END OF SHADOW.

HALFWAY BETWEEN MARKS

NORTH IS THIS WAY.

We love things that are quick and simple, ideas or gadgets that get a job done with a minimum of fuss. Sometimes we love their convenience so much that we're willing to overlook how poorly they actually work; so it is with the following.

All three techniques have been an accepted part of wayfinding lore for a long time. They work, but only under the rarest and best of circumstances—the rest of the time they offer only a crude approximation of direction. Try them yourself, checking the results against a compass (adjusted for declination).

South from a Watch

Point the hour hand of your watch at the sun, or line up the hour hand with a shadow from a vertical object. True south (true north in the Southern Hemisphere) should lie halfway between the hour hand and the number 12. (You should use the larger of the two arcs between the hour hand and 12 for measurements before 6 A.M. or after 6 P.M.; however, in those hours, you'd do as well or better to get a sunrise or sunset bearing, as we'll learn shortly.) If you have a digital watch, draw a clock's face in the dirt to represent an analog watch with the hour hand aimed as described.

Often ignored when explaining this technique is the need to correct for your longitude within the time zone (described on page 127) and for daylight saving time. But the biggest problem with this system is that the sun's bearing does not change at a constant rate—as does the clock's hour hand—throughout the day. The sun's apparent path through the sky varies with the season and latitude of the observer. While at times the results can be quite close, summer in the middle latitudes of the United States brings an average error of 20 degrees. This system works best closer to the poles and is almost useless in the tropics.

Following a Shadow

Place in the ground so that it is vertical a straight stick at least 3 feet long. Mark the end of its shadow. Wait at least 15 minutes until the end of the shadow has moved, and mark the new position. A line connecting the marks should run east and west, with your first mark being westernmost.

Unlike the watch-sun system, this one can get you reasonably close to an accurate direction. The principle is that as the sun moves westward, its shadow moves eastward. However, the sun's motion also has a northern component as it gains height in the morning and a southern component as it loses altitude in the afternoon, which can throw off your line. The sun is closest to moving directly westward around the sun's noon (not watch noon). Done within 2 hours of the sun's noon, you can get a direction that is accurate to within 10 degrees. The method is not reliable in the early morning or late afternoon, but it is accurate all day long at the time of the equinoxes (i.e., around March 21 and September 23).

Noon from a Shadow

You should be able to tell when it is noon because shadows are at their shortest then; technically, this is true. However, the change in length around midday is so slight compared with changes in the sun's bearing, which are quite rapid, that it is almost impossible to say exactly when noon occurs. It is this same fact that makes noon the best time for finding an east–west line by shadows, as described previously.

MOVEMENTS OF SUNRISE AND SUNSET

The sun doesn't always rise in the east and set in the west. In fact, it does this only twice a year: at the equinoxes, when the sun is over the equator, around March 21 and September 23. The rest of the year, the sun rises and sets north or south of east and west. For example, if you were just south of the Arctic Circle, there would be days when the sun rose far north of east, headed southward, and then returned to set far north of west. On those same days, someone on the equator would see the sun rise almost due east, pass almost overhead, and then set almost due west.

For most of us, the sun rises within a range of 30 degrees north or south of geographic east, giving a very rough but useful indication of direction. The sun's exact bearings depend on the time of year and your latitude (i.e., how far north or south of the equator you are).

In the Northern Hemisphere, after the fall equinox in late September, the sun rises farther to the south of east each day. It reaches its southernmost limit during the winter solstice, around December 21. By the spring equinox, in late March, the sun is rising directly in the east. From then on, it begins to rise farther to the north of east as each day passes, reaching its northernmost limit at the summer solstice around June 21. It then heads back toward the equator, rising ever closer to geographic east until the fall equinox (around September 23), when it comes up exactly in the east and sets exactly in the west.

This cycle can be used for a highly visible line of reference. While still in familiar surroundings, watch the sun for a few days, noting its position in the sky at different times. Get an idea of its bearings when it's rising and setting, and its height at midday. This pattern soon becomes part of your directional sense, sending a warning when you stray in the wrong direction.

How Long until Sunset?

Hold up your hand at arm's length and measure how many "fingers" the sun is above your visible horizon. Each horizontal finger equals about 15 minutes before sunset; therefore, four fingers equal about an hour. Using your other hand as well, eight fingers represent 2 hours—which is the limit of this trick unless you have an excess of digits.

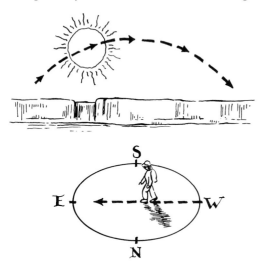

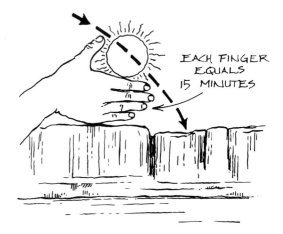

EACH FINGER EQUALS 15 MINUTES

BEARINGS FROM SUNRISE AND SUNSET

You can use the sun's rising and setting to get accurate bearings. Besides being helpful on their own, the bearings can be used to determine local declination by showing the difference between the sun's magnetic bearing (from the compass) and its geographic bearing as it comes up over the horizon. Don't worry if there isn't a clear horizon or you miss sunrise by a few minutes. At this time of day, the sun's bearing changes very slowly, about 1 degree every 8 minutes in Florida and every 4 minutes in northern Canada. So it can come up behind low hills or you can sleep a few minutes late, and you'll still get a reasonably accurate bearing.

Another handy item of information is that the amount the sun varies north or south of east upon rising is the same amount it varies from west when setting. If you know one, you know the other.

You can find the bearings of sunrise and sunset by using the circular chart on page 132, which was adapted from a chart published by David Burch, a master navigator, in his excellent book, *Emergency Navigation: Pathfinding Techniques for the Inquisitive and Prudent Mariner*. There's a blank version in the appendix that you can photocopy for your own calculations. The chart gives the sun's *amplitude*, or number of degrees north or south of 0 degrees (which represents due east or west). This is not the sun's bearing; to get that, you have to do some addition or subtraction. Just follow the step-by-step procedure to see how it's done.

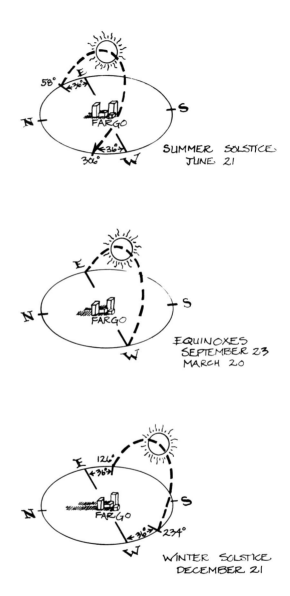

SUMMER SOLSTICE
JUNE 21

EQUINOXES
SEPTEMBER 23
MARCH 20

WINTER SOLSTICE
DECEMBER 21

Working Out the Bearings

1. Look up the sun's maximum amplitude (i.e., the farthest it travels north or south of 0 degrees during the year) at your latitude (an approximate latitude is fine). We'll use 47 degrees north, about right for Fargo, North Dakota, where the sun has a maximum amplitude of 36 degrees.
2. Scale the north–south baseline of the circular chart for 36 degrees on each side of the 0-degree mark. This can be accomplished by halving: halfway between 0 degrees and the circumference (which represents 36 degrees) is 18 degrees; mark that. Halfway between 0 degrees and 18 degrees is 9 degrees; mark that. Keep dividing each space on the baseline by half until you run out of room or get bored.
3. Find today's date along the circumference. Let's say it's August 1. Draw a line from the date toward and perpendicular to the baseline. Where

the lines intersect is the sun's amplitude for that day on that latitude. In this example, it's 27 degrees to the north of 0 degrees.
4. To find the sun's bearing when it rises, subtract north amplitude, or add south amplitude, to 90 degrees (east). In our example, we subtract 27 degrees from 90 degrees to get 63 degrees. When the sun rises, it will bear 063 degrees.
5. To find the sun's bearing when it sets, add north amplitude, or subtract south amplitude, from 270 degrees (west). In our example, we add 27 degrees to 270 degrees to get 297 degrees. When the sun sets, it will bear 297 degrees.

No one is expected to bring this chart along for use in an emergency; you do this before heading out, so that you have the sun's bearings when and if you need them. The bearings won't change much during the course of a week or within a few hundred miles north or south of where they were taken.

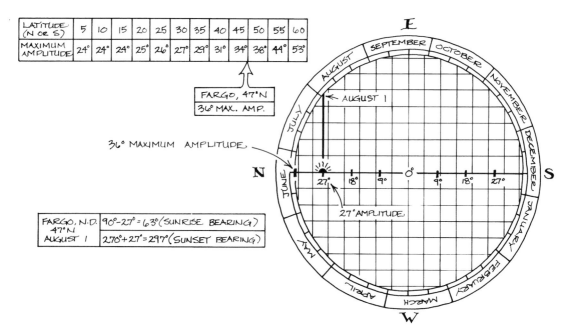

LATITUDE (N or S)	5	10	15	20	25	30	35	40	45	50	55	60
MAXIMUM AMPLITUDE	24°	24°	24°	25°	26°	27°	29°	31°	34°	38°	44°	53°

FARGO, 47°N
36° MAX. AMP.

36° MAXIMUM AMPLITUDE

FARGO, N.D. 47°N	90°−27° = 63° (SUNRISE BEARING)
AUGUST 1	270°+27° = 297° (SUNSET BEARING)

27° AMPLITUDE

POLARIS

Hiking at night is not advisable for beginners, except around the time of full moon when you are crossing clear, open ground. (With experience, you'll find that hiking trails at night isn't a problem, especially if you carry a good headlamp or flashlight.) It can be useful, however, to get bearings from the night sky—bearings you can use the next day. To make sense of the night sky, you'll do well to forget modern science and see the stars as folks did before Copernicus. Think of the heavens as the inside of a black bowl (the Polynesians saw it as a half-shell) with a fixed pattern of stars painted on it. While the earth stays still, this celestial bowl rotates around us once a day, using a line through the geographic north and south poles as its axis, with each star circling over us at a fixed latitude.

The handiest of all stars is Polaris, or the North Star, sitting almost at the bowl's axis directly over the north pole. This is a wonderful coincidence of nature, giving us a constant point of reference that never seems to move. Actually, it is not precisely over the pole, but rather rotates in a small counterclockwise orbit around it; however, the discrepancy is too small to be noticed by the naked eye and makes no difference for our purposes. In the tropics, Polaris begins to fall too close to the horizon for clarity. It becomes hard to spot south of 10 degrees north latitude, and disappears completely near the equator.

Another wonderful coincidence is that constellations rotating around Polaris can be used as pointers to help find it. This is helpful because Polaris is not a particularly bright star and doesn't stand out much in a crowd. The best indicators are the two "dippers." Polaris is the last star in the handle of the Little Dipper, which is not the easiest constellation to find. However, the Big Dipper is one of the most prominent constellations in the sky, and the stars that comprise the outer side of its cup act as pointers to Polaris. If you line up the star

Dubhe, at the cup's outer lip, with the star Merak, inside the cup, they make a straight line that runs directly to Polaris. The distance to Polaris along this line is five times that between Dubhe and Merak. It's useful to know the relationship between the two dippers: if water were poured from one, it would be caught in the other, and their handles bend in opposite directions.

If the Big Dipper is not visible, you can use Cassiopeia—a giant letter "W" or "M" (depending on the time of night) floating in the sky. If you were standing on Polaris, Cassiopeia would always look like an M. A perpendicular drawn from a line connecting the legs of the M and taken from the trailing leg hits Polaris at twice the M's width. If you can see the Big Dipper, Cassiopeia is across from it on the opposite side of Polaris. Incidentally, constellations revolve counterclockwise around Polaris.

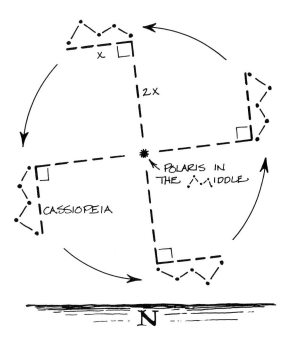

Latitude from Polaris

Polaris's height above an unimpeded horizon (i.e., no intervening hills or vegetation) gives us our approximate latitude. Ancient navigators knew the latitudes for all their destinations. They would sail, ride, or walk until Polaris showed that they were on that latitude, and then turn east or west toward their goal, keeping Polaris at the same height.

The "height" of the star is measured in degrees, the number of degrees equaling your latitude. Sailors use a sextant to ascertain this, but it's doubtful that you'll want to lug one of those around—although Major John Wesley Powell, John C. Fremont, and other Western explorers used them. Instead, you can use your fingers, sacrificing accuracy for convenience. Measure 10 degrees as shown, or hold your arm outstretched in front of you as if giving someone an enthusiastic "thumbs-up." The distance from the fleshy part of your hand (beneath the pinky joint) to the tip of your upstretched thumb is about 15 degrees. Now rotate your hand 90 degrees; the vertical distance represented by your thumb's width is 2 to 3 degrees. Rotate your hand again, so that your thumb points down; the distance from one knuckle to the next is about 3 degrees. You'll be lucky to get within a degree or two of your latitude, and every degree equals 60 miles, so this technique is of limited utility at best. However, these exercises somehow help us understand a proper relationship with the earth and heavens.

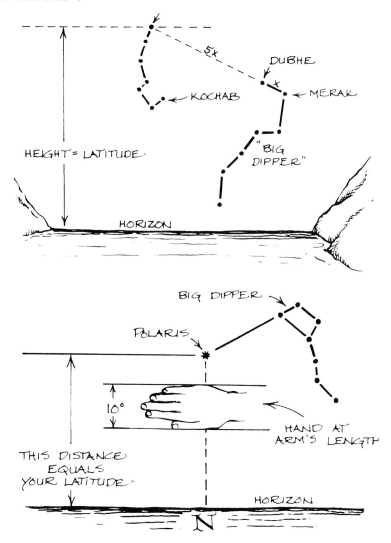

THE SOUTHERN CROSS

Good news and bad news; first, the good news. There's a star in the Southern Hemisphere comparable to Polaris, almost directly over the south pole. It's the star Sigma in the constellation Octans (which has no common name), and it will tell you which way is south.

The bad news is that the star is so dim as to be almost impossible to find with the naked eye, and it is surrounded by similar weak stars. But all is not lost. Again, as with Polaris, there are pointers to this star (or at least where this star would be if we could see it); in this case, in the constellation of the Southern Cross.

To many who see it for the first time, the Southern Cross is somewhat of a letdown. Compared with the northern pointers of Cassiopeia and the Big Dipper, it is small and unobtrusive. To some, its four brightest stars look more like a kite, because there is no star at the point where the two arms of the cross would intersect. There is also a nearby "False Cross," which has five stars.

However, the true cross can be confirmed by two closely spaced, very bright stars that trail behind the crosspiece. (Stars in the Southern Hemisphere travel clockwise around the pole.) These two stars are often easier to pick out than the cross itself. Look for them.

The long axis of the cross points to within 3 degrees of the celestial south pole—not an exact pointer, but very close. The distance is four-and-a-half times the long axis of the cross from its bottom.

The Southern Cross is visible as far north as 25 degrees of latitude, but only for short periods during the night. Its use as a navigational aid is limited north of the equator because the celestial south pole then lies below the horizon. The only time it is a good indicator of south is when the cross appears to be vertical.

The farther you head south from the equator, the longer the Southern Cross stays above the horizon, and from 37 degrees south latitude southward, it remains visible throughout the night.

The toe of the stargazer is often stubbed.

—Russian proverb

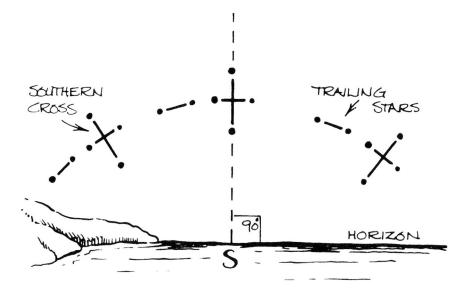

OTHER STARS

Observed Motion of Any Star

Here's a way to get directions when identifying individual stars is impossible. It is based on the principle that stars travel from east to west.

Sight on any star in mid-sky (stay away from stars near the poles) and note its position relative to something on the ground (e.g., a treetop, peak, or nearby stick you have planted for the purpose). Give the star about 20 minutes and see which way it travels. If it heads downward, it's in the west; if it goes upward, it's in the east. If it goes to the right, it's in the south; if it goes to the left, it's in the north.

Orion

Highly visible in the winter sky (or summer sky in the Southern Hemisphere), Orion circles the earth on the celestial equator. The leading and northernmost star in its belt is actually on the equator and, therefore, rises in the east and sets in the west regardless from which latitude you see it.

Because you may not remember which is the correct star or be able to pick out the one that is leading or northernmost, use the middle star—the belt's "buckle"—which is only 1 degree from the equator.

It is easier to find west with Orion than it is to find east. Wait until the constellation begins to set and then see where the "buckle" touches the horizon. To find east, you have to know what the constellation looks like emerging from below the horizon or, once up, how to retrace the buckle's path back to where it popped up. Both are hard to do.

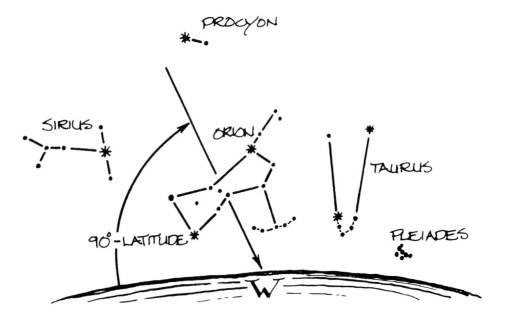

The Shadow Knows

The fact that the sun rises in the east and sets in the west is a basic navigational tool. During the day, the sun should be as valuable to you as your compass. Even in situations where the sun is obscured by canyon walls, shadows point you in the right direction. As a wilderness ranger in the canyon country of Utah, I used the sun almost exclusively for my navigation. Of course, I always kept my map and compass handy while on patrol, but it was a thrill to confirm that your estimates using the sun were right on or real close.

The sun would play tricks on me down in the canyons. Anasazi ruins dot the vertical landscape throughout southeastern Utah, and I discovered that the ancient ones used the sun and shadows to their advantage for warmth and concealment. On every patrol, I combed the walls while hiking, looking for signs of ruins. Funny thing was, even though I might have already been through a section of canyon, depending on the light, I might spot a ruin I had never seen before.

As for navigating, that was easy. To determine which section of canyon I was in, I would watch to see the direction of the shadows. If the sun struck a wall first, then that wall was west. If the sun rose at either end of the canyon, then that was east. In the evening, the last rays of light on the higher canyon walls indicated east–west orientation as well. What do you do when the sun is directly overhead? That's simple: find some shade and have lunch.

PJC

7

EXTREME ENVIRONMENTS

MOUNTAINS

Regardless of where you are, you'll be able to use and adapt the information in the preceding chapters. So-called extreme environments may be comparatively easy to navigate even if they are hard to traverse. Mountains are just such places.

If anything, navigating in mountains is somewhat easier than on level terrain because of the numerous visible landmarks—most notably, mountain peaks. Even when conditions are unfavorable, it is often more difficult to get lost in mountains. To get disoriented, you usually have to climb out of one river drainage and into another—more often than not, a hard-to-miss transition.

Of course, there are some adjustments to make when you take your navigating skills to the vertical world of mountains and steep hill country. Distances taken directly from a map are misleading because they read as if the landscape had been flattened. One "map" mile between two points could very well turn out to be nearer two "real-world" miles over steep terrain. To better understand this, review the sections of chapter 2 on Distance, Slope Profiles, and Slope Gradients.

If the contour lines on your topo map leave you in any doubt, or you have only a planimetric map (i.e., without contour lines), a sure sign of steeply rising land is a trail with a series of switchbacks or hairpin turns on your map—the only route a trail can take to avoid a difficult direct climb. However, most often, maps are not so obvious in their clues. Unless you are used to map-reading in alpine areas, you'll be astounded at how much bigger and steeper the mountains actually are. You may be good at interpreting contour lines, but there is little in most people's experience to help make the transition from hills to mountains.

Compasses are also better suited to level going. Try this for yourself: take a bearing of your neighbor's chimney from your backyard. It doesn't take much of an upward angle to bind up the needle until it is no longer free to swing. In practice, though, this really isn't a problem. If you're close enough to a cliff, peak, or other landmark that you have to crane your neck upward for a bearing, you probably don't need the bearing to navigate. If you do, simply take a bearing off the base of the landmark; it will be accurate enough.

In general, you have less need for constant reference to your compass in the mountains than on level ground because of the prominent landmarks. In fact, you seldom keep actual "courses." You generally head somewhere specific, such as a pass or peak, and leave from a natural feature, such as a riverside meadow or a canyon-bottom trailhead. The trail or unmarked route simply follows the line of least resistance while you read the lay of the land. The path up a steep slope often turns in switchbacks to reduce the grade—so you are continually changing directions and at no time are you heading directly toward your goal. When you can't keep your destination in sight, you may find it helpful to use intermediate landmarks.

Upon reaching a summit, you usually can orient yourself by comparing the surrounding high points with peaks shown on your map. Use compass bearings as necessary to put things into perspective. Use elevation information—if the map shows your elevation, compare that with peaks above or below your horizontal line of sight. Use the tree line or snow line to help gauge the height of other mountains. In areas where the vegetation changes predictably and dramatically with elevation, you can use those clues to estimate the heights of various landmarks. If you are confused during the climb, don't worry—as you gain height, landmarks become fewer, more obvious, and more easily identified.

Once you have arrived at the summit, make careful plans for your descent. It is much easier to get disoriented going down toward the rest of the world than going up to a small point in the sky. Take advantage of the spectacular view around you to choose your route. Look for landmarks, turning points, and big clues that indicate you are off course. Think about aiming off, and identify naturally occurring brackets. It's a good idea to make notes on the map to which you can refer as you descend, but few people do this. In stormy weather or dense clouds—just the conditions when routefinding is difficult—making notes is impossible. It is better to work out compass bearings in advance for a handy reference when required.

An Arduous Lesson

Swathed in glaciers, Mt. Baker in northwestern Washington State is more than a mountain covered in snow—it's a volcano surrounded by a maze of ice. Navigation through the crevasse-filled glaciers to get near the mountain is extreme, to say the least. There is no route to the summit that doesn't cross the hazardous glaciers and, to make matters worse, Mt. Baker is also usually socked in with clouds that obscure landmarks. That's where we were when a small group of friends and I got a lesson in extreme navigation.

We knew a storm was going to roll in but had decided that it wouldn't stop us. It was a beautiful blue-sky Saturday during a stretch of Indian summer. Our plan was to get as high as we could and, if it stormed on us too badly, we would just bail. We negotiated through the vast crevasse-crossed ice fields under the hot sun. By the time we reached camp that evening, the clouds had rolled in and the first flurries had started.

That night, the wind literally pounded the tent so flat that most of the time the fabric was on our faces. In the morning, we took a look outside and decided that this was not the day to go for the summit. Problem was that our route back down to the trailhead was just as obscured as the route to the summit. Between us and our vehicles lay countless crevasses that don't allow for straight-line travel. We packed our soaked gear and began our slow and arduous descent.

We had placed no wands of any sort (see page 143) and none of us was that familiar with the mountain, so we took turns choosing the route through the glacier. We knew we had to descend a couple thousand feet and work our way southwest to reach a place where the glacier and moraine met at a point we could easily traverse. It was also where we had to pick up the trail again. The rain was blowing sideways as we continued our descent. What should have taken a couple of hours turned into a full day of epic navigating. Since then, I have always carried and used wands to plant in the snow to mark the trail during whiteouts on peaks like Mt. Baker with a great deal of success.

PJC

Altimeters and GPS Receivers

Sometimes it is difficult to take bearings of or from a shrouded summit. Wouldn't it be nice if there were some other instrument to help mountaineers find their way? Actually, there are two.

The *altimeter* is nothing more than a portable barometer, an instrument that measures air pressure. The principle is that as you go up, air pressure (i.e., the weight of the air) decreases at a uniform rate. As you descend, it increases. Therefore, if you calibrate a barometer to read these changes in pressure as feet (or meters), you can always determine your elevation. And that's a good thing to know.

If you're sure you're at 1,800 feet, then you must be somewhere along the 1,800-foot contour line—which eliminates a lot of real estate. That contour line provides an excellent line of position that can be crossed with a bearing or a natural feature (e.g., a trail, ridge, stream, or notch) to give you a fix. Unfortunately, uncontrollable factors can throw off an altimeter's readings; that is, changes in temperature and variations in air pressure caused by weather.

The heart of an altimeter is a metal capsule that encloses a partial vacuum. The surrounding air pressure forces the capsule to expand and contract, and this movement is connected either to a pointer that moves along a scale or to a digital readout. But the capsule also flexes under changes of temperature, thereby causing false readings.

The best defense is to prevent temperature variations. Carry your altimeter in an outside pack pocket rather than in a shirt pocket so it stays at the same temperature as the ambient air. And don't expect an altimeter adjusted in a warm cabin to be accurate out on the glacier. Temperature problems can be almost eliminated by using a temperature-compensated altimeter, but the convenience and precision cost you more—around $200 in 2001.

Then there is weather, about which no one can do anything. It's possible to go to sleep with the altimeter displaying one height and wake up in the morning to have it read a significantly different one. Your tent didn't levitate—all it takes is a shift in the barometric pressure to make you think the altimeter (or you) has gone nuts. This can be even more puzzling when you are underway. You won't be able to differentiate between the effects of the changing altitude and meteorological changes, which makes a complete guessing game of your elevation.

The best way to get accurate readings is to adjust the altimeter every chance you get. Each time you come to or are about to leave from a position that has its elevation noted on the map, check the altimeter; then reset it if necessary. To minimize the effect of weather changes, try to make these adjustments at least once an hour.

Whether altimeters are worth the effort or expense is up to you. Some climbers swear by them; others—probably the majority—swear *at* them.

For not much more than a good altimeter, you can buy a global positioning system (GPS) receiver, which fixes your position and your altitude, and can be used in fog, darkness, and your tent. (See chapter 8 for more information.)

SNOW

Snow changes things, filling in the landscape like spackle on cheap wallboard. Areas exposed to windblown snow develop new and ever-changing contours. Depressions are leveled out; drifts fill ravines, turning them into flats; and ground characteristics such as rocks and vegetation are covered. Trails disappear, blazes and signs are hidden, and bodies of water look like open fields. Some of the subtle indicators you depend on during the warmer months are gone—but the principal landmarks and the principles of magnetic navigation remain.

An all-white environment reduces depth perception and judgment of distances, which is made worse by the low contrast of weak light from gray winter skies or the snow blindness caused by dazzling sun. In general, however, snow poses more problems to travel than to navigation. You will encounter three main types of terrain in snow, each posing its own navigational problems.

The first is rolling wooded lowlands or foothills on the fringe of a mountain range. This terrain provides little in the way of direction-finding clues. Slopes may be exaggerated or softened by drifting snow so that in some areas the contour lines deceive as much as they inform. In this case, look to the more up-to-date portrayal of back roads that you can usually find on the planimetric maps distributed by the U.S. Forest Service, Land Management Bureau, and local parks. Knowing where these roads are and where they lead to can be a godsend. Of course, when handling any type of map, remember that all that cold white stuff is only water in disguise—get it on a map warmed in your pocket and you have a map that won't last much longer. The solution is to use a transparent waterproof map case or to treat your map with one of the waterproofing compounds available for the purpose. Alternatively, if one is available for the region you're visiting, use a map printed on waterproof plastic, such as those from *Trails Illustrated* (see the appendix).

Trail-marking cairns are likely to be blanketed, and when snow is on the trees, blazes may be hidden as well. In general, only the higher and more obvious landmarks will be visible, and these may be rare in this terrain. One of the few remaining natural references is a fast-flowing river or stream that rarely freezes over, which can make a good line of position or baseline. However, following it can be hazardous—a section covered by snow may collapse if you inadvertently venture onto it. Also, streams always take the quickest way downhill, leading you to steep, dangerous slopes. Large frozen lakes and rivers are also good position indicators and can be excellent "highways" upon which to travel and make good time, but you must be extremely wary of thin ice. Navigating on large lakes can be very difficult, however, when you can't see either shore due to a whiteout or blizzard. And because the wind can create large drifts, snow-covered lakes are not always flat.

The second frequently encountered terrain is the subalpine area below the tree line, where your best guides and routes to follow are along the valleys, canyons, and ravines that have not been filled in. Knowing the direction in which a valley runs may be enough to keep you from getting lost (as long as you really are in the valley you *think* you're in). Do this by keeping constant track of your route. Do not depend on the prevailing winds as a reference in this type of landscape—they will be twisted by the land, coming at you from all directions each time you turn a corner.

The third area of travel in snow country is the high alpine zone above the tree line—the domain of the mountaineer and the ski tourer. Here, your greatest enemy is the snow in the air, as well as that on the ground. Know where you are at all times because visibility can deteriorate quite suddenly. At the first sign of an approaching snowstorm or when dense clouds start to form, pinpoint your position with bearings on a map. As the weather closes in, look for large dark shadows in the misty whiteout to use as intermediate landmarks along the way. A heavy snowfall can obscure all clues rapidly. There is also the danger of your suffering from vertigo in a world where there is no clear demarcation between sky and ground.

Sometimes it is difficult to know whether you are moving up or down. One useful trick is to throw a snowball ahead of you: if it appears stuck in midair, the ground ahead must slope upward; if it lands lower than your feet, you are on a downward slope and need to proceed very carefully. If it disappears from view, back off quickly; you could be on a cornice or the edge of a steep drop.

Thankfully, whiteouts are not that common, but they are certainly treacherous when you're traveling near crevasses. Plan escape routes in case of bad weather, or be equipped and prepared to camp or snow-hole until the weather clears. Even if you could travel a reliable compass course, don't do it—you could walk straight into a crevasse. In a pinch, you might be able to retrace your tracks if the wind has not obliterated them, but this can be tedious and dangerous if you can only see a few feet ahead. You may also wind up following someone else's tracks.

When the weather is good, dead-reckoning techniques work well even on glaciers or other open snowfields—*most* of the time. But for intricate routes on crevassed glaciers lacking reliable landmarks, you need greater navigation precision than dead reckoning provides, which means you have to make your own guides. All the information in chapter 3 about how to follow a straight course when there are no landmarks applies here. Look it over now. You can use back bearings or even other members of your party. But one of the best ways is to make your own transit markers using wands that you carry along for that purpose.

These wands are often made of lightweight, split-bamboo poles with strips of cloth tied to them. You can make them yourself from green bamboo sticks sold as plant supports at garden supply stores. Slit the top a few inches, slide in any brightly colored durable material, tie it in place, and then tape the top of the wand shut. Make everything strong. Wands should be 36 to 48 inches long. If you need wands at all, chances are you need a lot of them.

Wands can be used as transits to help you keep a straight course or as trail markers for your return trip. When used as the latter, make sure you space them closely enough that the next marker comes into view as the last member of your party passes the previous one. Under no circumstances should the last person leave a wand before the new one has been positively sighted. Then, and only then, is that previous wand collected for later use, so as not to leave a maze of old and potentially confusing trails. Tilt wands to point toward the next one along. Don't place them in hollows or on the downside of a ridge where they will be hard to see on the way back. Mark important wands—those that indicate course changes or dangers—differently. The standard sign for a crevasse or danger is two crossed wands.

Finally, ski tourers and mountaineers need to know how to recognize potential avalanche danger both on the map and on the ground. Avalanches usually occur on slopes of 25 to 45 degrees. If in doubt, stay off steep slopes. Ridges are safer, as are wide valley bottoms. Watch for avalanche chutes such as tree-free corridors on forested mountainsides, and don't camp below them! Snow travelers should study this subject well (there are several good books on the subject—see the appendix), know how to dig test pits, and know what to do if an avalanche occurs.

Now, for a change of pace, here's a little quiz. Which of the following four pieces of folklore are true?

- Snow tends to be finer and less granular on the northern side of ridges, trees, and other prominent features.
- In winter, poplar trees are darker on their northern sides.
- Solitary coniferous trees are bushiest on their southern sides.
- Northern slopes are less densely packed with snow, but are icier.

Well, how did you do? Here's the answer: Trust none of the above. Take all the precautions that you can when traveling in snow. Those gentle flakes can be killers when they gang up on you.

DESERTS

The deserts of the American Southwest are one of the toughest environments in which to navigate—*much* more difficult than mountains, for example. This is mostly due to the presence of canyons and *arroyos* (i.e., deep washes), which tend to obstruct your path quite suddenly. Because they cut into the topography rather than rising above it, the flat, open plain or tableland you thought to cross can stop you cold with little advance warning. Often, you have to plot avoidance bearings for unseen canyons, then skirt them via compass bearings (as discussed in chapter 4).

The popular image of a desert paints it as a vast, open space; however, many, such as the Colorado Plateau, are extremely convoluted in their topography. We think of deserts as fields of sand dunes, yet sand dunes are a novelty in America's deserts. We think of deserts as flat, yet the canyonlands of the Southwest have more vertical terrain than most mountain ranges. And we tend to think of deserts as barren, yet some, such as the Sonoran Desert, are anything but that. In the flat Sonoran terrain, obscuring vegetation such as mesquite and paloverde trees makes sighting on distant landmarks difficult.

Nevertheless, bearings on distant landmarks are the staple of desert navigation. Often, there is a lack of notable features in the foreground, but there is a circle of larger (and often quite striking) landmarks in the far distance.

Be cautious before taking those first steps from the trailhead or base camp. Distances in the clear, dry air are deceptive. Mountains that appear to be only a few miles off in actuality may be 20 or 30 miles away; distances across wide valleys are even harder to judge. Your goal could be in view yet still take many days to reach. An oft-quoted rule-of-thumb for desert travel is to multiply your estimated distance by a factor of three to compensate for natural underestimation.

Once out there, look to those bold, distant features, using bearings from your compass and information from recently updated topo maps. One of the more confusing aspects of desert travel is the mazelike network of back roads passing through it. The less substantial roads get blown away or washed out, and many that seem quite good are not included on the map. Checking with local land-management agents and rangers before using a map is a good way to find out the current status of those constantly changing roads. When following a road, keep meticulous track of each turnoff, fork, junction, direction turned, and mileage covered. Because there are rarely any road signs in the desert, this is the only way to know where you are. And that's important, because one wrong turn can lead into a bewildering network of back roads from which there seems to be no way out. In the desert, as in any extreme environment, caution and preparation are the keys to finding your way.

The canyon country does not always inspire love. To many it appears barren, hostile, repellent—a fearsome land of rock and heat, sand dunes and quicksand, cactus, thornbush, scorpion, rattlesnake, and agoraphobic distances. To those who see our land in that manner, the best reply is, yes, you are right, it is a dangerous and terrible place. Enter at your own risk. Carry water. Avoid the noonday sun. Try to ignore the vultures. Pray frequently.

—Edward Abbey,
The Journey Home

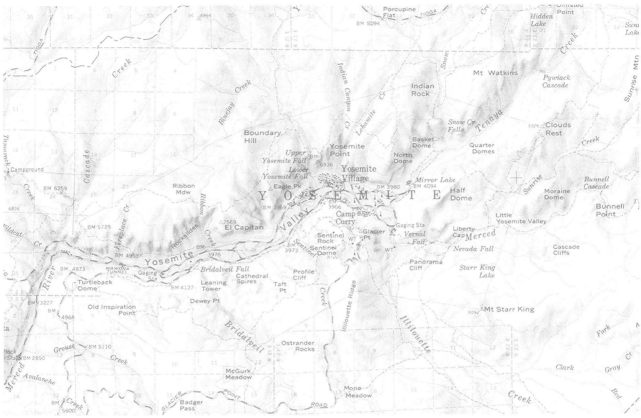

Think global, hike local, because the global positioning system (GPS) puts the world at your fingertips. There's no doubt that the GPS has changed the way hikers and mariners navigate. A GPS receiver the size of a cell phone can pinpoint your position virtually anywhere on the earth—at any time, in any weather—to within about 10 to 30 meters. A GPS receiver can tell you what course to follow to arrive at your destination, and then guide you back to where you started. It is compact enough to strap to a kayak, a canoe, a mountain bike, or to even jam in your pocket.

Many GPS receivers allow you to store route-finding coordinates of your best-held-secret spots. GPS allows you to securely find your way in the fog or a blizzard, across a flat desert devoid of recognizable landmarks, and through a thick forest at night.

So is the GPS the gift that will get the masses into the Great Outdoors, that great democratizer? Hardly. If you don't have a firm grasp of navigational essentials, if you don't understand basic map and compass skills, the only place a GPS receiver will lead you is into a great deal of trouble.

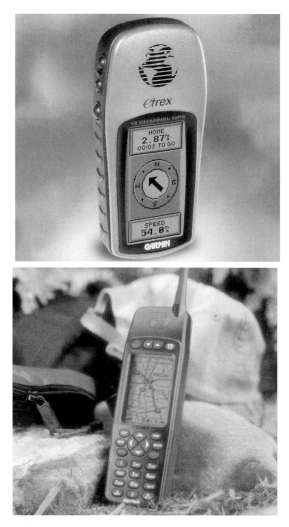

Handheld GPS units vary not just by electronic features but by size, weight, waterproofness, and complexity so you can find the model that best meets your needs.

Without map and compass skills—indeed, without a map and compass to complement your GPS information—having a GPS-inspired bearing to follow to your destination won't do you any good. This is pointedly true in the wilderness, where an impenetrable swamp, sheer cliff, or raging stream might lie in wait between you and your destination. To be accurate, a GPS must get readings from at least four satellites. If you're sitting under a cliff or under a thick canopy of tree cover—not a totally unusual circumstance in the wilderness—you can't get an accurate reading. A GPS receiver can tell you how to get there and how to get back, but it can't tell you what lies in wait.

And GPS receivers, like any other appliance, are far from indestructible. Drop one in the aforementioned stream and you might be truly up the river without a paddle—or off a cliff without a parachute. And what about the batteries you need to keep it running? You get the picture.

The GPS is a truly wonderful tool, but it should never be relied on as your primary source of navigation. Like anything else that promises instant gratification, you'll feel more confident when you know the satisfaction of mastering map and compass skills.

Combine the information from the previous chapters and a handheld GPS receiver and you'll never be lost. However, a cell phone and GPS unit do not constitute skill and experience. Never travel without a working compass, detailed maps, spare batteries, and some local knowledge. GPS technology places a premium on the skills discussed in chapters 1 through 6 to calculate the precise latitude and longitude of your chosen landmarks, and then enter that information accurately into your GPS receiver. For this, you need to know how to identify key terrain features (e.g., a cliff or swamp) and locate them on your map. Make an error in calculating the exact location of some place you really need to avoid, like Deadman's Gulch, and your handy new GPS receiver may just steer you into the debacle you wanted to avoid.

GPS units can disgorge a bewildering array of information: precise location, average speed, distance traveled, distances and bearings to all types of landmarks, the position of navigational aids (e.g., lighthouses and buoys), altitude, precise time, and more. A hiker can mark the location of camp, the trailhead, and interesting destinations along the way. A sailor can chart a course from isle to isle, avoiding shoals along the way—and then follow the route in pea-soup fog without incident. Some units even beep insistently when you near your destination or when you stray from your course. Since the first GPS unit for civilians hit the market in the late 1980s, manufacturers have steadily improved and modified their offerings—making them smaller, more versatile, and more accurate—and integrating communication features such as PC compatibility and downloadable CD-ROM topographic maps. They're also a lot cheaper: the first units available to the public ran around $3,000; now you can get everything you need for under $100.

Technology Sans Sense

As in many classic tales of learning through experience, the main character of this one has a pseudonym, although I can't resist revealing that I'm related to "Chris" by marriage. Chris had years of trail miles before this incident took place, so inexperience was no excuse for getting lost.

Chris grabbed a day pack, tossed in a newly purchased GPS receiver, and headed out for a sunny day in the mountains without a care in the world. Chris disregarded many of his (or her) hard-earned wilderness skills and just went crashing into the forest. The brand-new GPS unit meant he didn't need a map or compass—the GPS would do all the work, right?

A couple hours into the hike, Chris realized (1) he didn't have a clue as to where he was going and (2) he should have brought the GPS instructions to figure out how to check where he had been. So Chris kept going, which is another classic thing lost people do to become even more lost. After a period of bewilderment, Chris crossed the path of a pair of hikers with a map and compass, and they steered Chris in the right direction. I haven't heard any hiking tales from Chris since.

PJC

GPS 101

The GPS depends on signals from a satellite system funded by the U.S. government (that means you) and operated by the U.S. Department of Defense (DOD). Its military usefulness is manifold, and the system's most sophisticated applications can locate troops and ships or bomb strikes with startling accuracy.

As with other technologies developed for the military, the GPS has exceptionally useful civilian applications as well. The system, begun in the early 1970s and fully operational by the mid-1990s, depends on a constellation of twenty-four satellites orbiting the earth at an altitude of some 12,000 miles. The satellites are constantly monitored by five ground stations at different points around the world, which confirm data from a fixed location.

GPS Basics

Simply put, each of the operating satellites in the system continuously transmits time-coded signals back to earth, which your GPS receiver uses to calculate your location. These signals contain information on the satellite's orbit (i.e., position, altitude, and speed), time, and position relative to other GPS satellites. The information is offered on two levels. The more accurate one, Precision Positioning Service (PPS, or P-Code), is available only for military use. The less accurate one, Standard Positioning Service (SPS, or C/A-Code), is available to anyone in the world with a GPS receiver. Until May 1, 2000, the SPS code was subject to *Selective Availability (SA),* a process by which the government randomly degraded the signal and thus its accuracy. As of May 1, 2000, the U.S. government says it has stopped the practice of SA, although it reserves the right to reinstate it at any time. This, of course, is based on fears that an enemy could use the accuracy of GPS against U.S. armed forces (during a war, the DOD could effectively shut down the entire system). Few wilderness navigators need the extreme precision demanded by the military and, for all practical purposes, the system is plenty accurate even when SA is in effect.

Your GPS receiver reads signals from multiple satellites and determines the time it took each signal to travel, calculating its distance from each satellite using a simple equation: speed of the radio signal (velocity) multiplied by the precise time it took the signal to travel equals distance. Knowing the distance, the receiver can triangulate (i.e., algorithmically compute) its position.

Getting a Fix

The satellites and the master ground station are equipped with precise atomic clocks; your inexpensive GPS receiver is not. Because the calculations are based on very precise time, the receiver must be able to achieve atomic-clock accuracy. By locking onto multiple satellites, geometry and logic allow the receiver's computer to determine a time-correction factor and automatically resynchronize. For a three-dimensional fix that provides longitude, latitude, and altitude, at least four satellites are required. If trees, canyon walls, or mountains—among other obstacles—obscure the satellite signals, the receiver may be unable to access enough satellites to get all the information it needs, thereby providing only latitude-longitude coordinates. This is called a *2-D position fix.* Newer handheld GPS units are able to get a lock on eight to twelve satellites above the horizon at any one time.

Another factor affecting GPS accuracy is satellite geometry or, in simple terms, where the satellites are located relative to each other from the receiver's perspective—it's the same geometry problem you have when making a fix from visual sightings on the ground (see illustration page 100). Say, for instance, that you are locked onto four satellites, but they are all orbiting north and west of you. An accurate fix on your position may be impossible because of poor triangulation on signals coming from the same general direction. This type of situation could place you off by as much as a half-mile. If those same four satellites are orbiting at approximately 90-degree intervals north, east, south, and west, accuracy improves dramatically. Because the measurements are coming from all directions, the common area where they all intersect is much smaller.

If satellite signals bounce off terrain features such as a sheer rock face or large snow or ice fields before reaching the receiver's antenna, they take longer, which fools the GPS into thinking that the satellite is farther away than it actually is. Fortunately, errors from multipathing rarely put your known position off by more than a few dozen feet, unless you're near a large, highly reflective surface such as a rock face.

Types of Receivers

There are two types of receivers available on today's market: *parallel channel* and *multiplexing*. A parallel-channel receiver is the industry standard and what you want. It increases the chances of getting a lock on enough satellites to get a position fix because the receiver maintains a constant lock on each satellite. When buying a GPS receiver, remember that just because a unit can track eight to twelve satellites does not make it a twelve-parallel-channel receiver. Some of the older models can track that many satellites but only process the information from one satellite at a time in a very time-consuming process. A multiplexing receiver is less costly and merely samples satellite data without ever locking on, so it tends to be a little less accurate. A multiplexing receiver also has limitations when it comes to finding and maintaining satellite contact due to heavy foliage and obstructions.

As with so many other technological electronic gizmos, the price of a GPS receiver varies according to the level of accuracy offered. Competition has driven prices down and the number of useful features up. All GPS units should have a convenient way to input and display information. Most outdoor enthusiasts find that a basic handheld GPS, around $100, is perfectly suitable. These units are durable, waterproof, compact, and lightweight, and provide days of service on just a couple of AA batteries. Even at this price, you can find units with a twelve-parallel-channel receiver, the ability to upload and download waypoints, and the ability to work with PC-based map software. Usually referred to as *nonmapping units*, they do not come with built-in maps, databases, cartridges, or the ability to download a CD-ROM map into the GPS unit.

The next step up is the *mapping unit*. In addition to all the features of the basic GPS receivers, this receiver may include built-in maps or databases that display as a base map, or a background map. This receiver includes the ability to download much more detailed mapping data from optional topographic and marine-chart CD-ROMs and data cartridges,

making them a more attractive option for serious waterhounds. And all that great information isn't confined to a tiny screen; when interfaced with a PC, the GPS receiver can provide large, colorful, detailed map displays.

As the price increases, so do the features and options. External enhancements might include units with larger color display screens and higher resolution, extended operating temperature ranges, extended operating time (i.e., the unit holds more batteries) and/or rechargeable batteries, and extended external power-source range. (For example, some less costly units cannot handle the voltage from the lighter attachment.) Expect to pay a little more to have an internal back-up battery (i.e., lithium) to protect that precious or hard-won data you have stored in memory. Check into which accessories are included or available. A key desirable option is whether the built-in antenna can be detached. A detachable antenna allows for less jarring and the receiver can be secured in a pack or case for mountain biking, paddling, and driving; it can be more conveniently mounted for a direct-signal connection.

Internal enhancements center around the unit's ability to access more information and to customize, display, store, and transmit it. This means more memory to store waypoints, routes, legs, and backtracks. Also, built-in thermometers and altimeters and electronic compasses are nice. You can store more global coordinates and map datum ranges, built-in databases, interchangeable databases, and information such as sunrise, sunset, and tide-table almanacs.

Some marine GPS systems, for example, have alarms that warn you when you are nearing your destination or danger such as a reef or a shoal. For wilderness use, you have the option of endless customizing. For example, waypoint messaging allows you to enter text associated with a waypoint (e.g., "Look left here!"), or to use a little tent icon to mark the camping waypoints and a little skull and crossbones for danger waypoints. A number of manufacturers offer waypoint data management software (not to be confused with maps!) and helpful users offer free data-management programs for downloading off the Web. These programs allow for customization of data transfer, create and edit waypoints and routes, and coordinate conversion.

GETTING STARTED

Start-Up and Screens

Most handheld GPS receivers are relatively easy to set up and operate. Instructions and user guides are easy to follow and get you started, provided you read them. Most manufacturers have manuals available online. These instructions include basics such as battery information, initial position, and how to input a destination.

It's a good idea to get to know how your GPS receiver works before heading out into the woods. You would look mighty ridiculous if the search-and-rescue team realized that you had a working GPS and cell phone but you couldn't operate the GPS, so you called them away from their warm homes for a little backwoods tutorial.

Before you head out into the wilderness with your new GPS unit, it's a good idea to *initialize it*. This is merely the process of turning on a new receiver and entering local time and location for a speedy lock on satellites; or you can let it get a fix by itself for a longer *cold start*. Before initializing, it is essential to coordinate your coordinates; that is, make sure your reference map and GPS receiver are set to use the same position format (e.g., latitude and longitude, UTM) and map datum (check the map collar). Set the declination of your GPS unit and compass the same. To initialize, you need to enter your approximate current position in latitude and longitude; approximate elevation, or altitude; and the current local time and date. Normally, initialization is necessary only once, provided the GPS receiver stays within about 300 miles of where it was last turned off.

The position screen indicates which satellites the GPS unit is locked onto, how strong the signal is, and where they are in orbit relative to where you are standing. Every GPS receiver is programmed with a satellite almanac (i.e., schedule) so that once initialized, it knows by the orbit almanac which satellites should be overhead. The position screen usually displays location, elevation, and time. Like a TV satellite dish, it's best to have a clear, unobstructed path to receive a signal. However, once you have locked on to a signal, it is best to leave the unit on if you are hiking in obscured terrain (e.g., a forest or a canyon). It is easier for the GPS to maintain a signal than to reacquire one.

Waypoints and Routes

A *waypoint* is a specific position or location stored in the unit's memory for future use, such as the coordinates of the trailhead so that if you bail on the trip, you can always get back to the vehicle. Waypoints can be entered manually from a map or other source (e.g., guidebook or the Web), or downloaded, transmitted, or taken in the field from a position fix. Some receivers allow you to attach an icon or text to the waypoint.

A *route* is a series of waypoints strung together to make an electronic path that also represents the trail you intend to follow. Each segment between the waypoints is called a *leg*.

At the start of the trip, you select the route you intend to follow and enter that data into the GPS unit. The receiver then tells you the distance and bearing you need to follow to reach the next waypoint. However, a compass and map are mandatory. This all occurs on the navigation screen, which also tells you if you are on course or, if you're not, how far off you are and which direction to turn to get back on course. Some navigation screens show your heading (i.e., the direction you are moving in), but not if you are not moving!

Remember that the GPS bearings travel in a straight line; if you need to hike around an obstacle, then you need to program the route as such, waypoint to waypoint. Make sure that each waypoint on the route keeps you clear of the danger as you head to the next. Again, map-reading skills are critical for programming the correct data into your GPS (see chapter 2). If you can't read a map correctly and can't tell the GPS unit where you want to go, then how can it help you?

Using your receiver's plotter screen mode, you get a bird's-eye view of the trail you have followed and a visual indication of the route you need to follow. Some higher-end GPS receivers are able to download real topo maps for display on the plotting screen. Create trails on this screen by tracking, manually or automatically collecting position points (i.e., dropping electronic bread crumbs), and saving them for quick backtracking purposes or to come back on another trip.

E-MAPS: TOPOS AND CHARTS ON CD-ROM

Another recent technological innovation—digital maps on CD-ROM—has opened up new ways to utilize your home computer for adventure beyond the walls of your house. Digital mapping applications turn GPS position readouts into a meaningful visual. The industry behind these products is progressing so rapidly that the handheld PC–CD-ROM map unit–GPS receiver–cell-phone combination will be available within a couple of years. For now, the interaction between the CD-ROM map sets and GPS receivers is somewhat limited, and the computer-based maps are—for the most part—currently stuck on the computer. The revolution in mapping, the palm-sized PCs, and wireless technology will play in integral part in the next generation of navigational tools.

What to Look For

A number of digital map products are currently on the market, such as those sold by Delorme, Map-Tech, TopoUSA, and Wildflower. You can expect to pay anywhere from $40 up to $200. There are several manufacturers of specific CD maps for national parks, with a wide range of quality. These map sets cover individual trails, counties, states, and regions of the country, or the entire United States or world. Fantastic detailed maps are available using the USG 7.5-Minute-Series Topographic 1:24,000-scale Quadrangle maps. The software should include these basic features:

- The ability to pan across the maps easily: look for seamless maps (not all manufacturers have them) that allow you access to adjacent map sheets displayed as one continuous topographic map
- Different resolution settings allowing the user to find a point and zoom in to get a better picture
- GPS interface support that includes the ability to upload and download waypoint, track, and route information
- A find or search function, or a searchable index that includes place names, feature names, and coordinates
- Tools for annotating maps with points of inter-

est, routes, text, and icons, and the ability to save the customized maps
- Tools for calculating elevation gain-loss, distance, bearings, and headings
- The ability to generate terrain profiles along any path the user defines
- The ability to upload topo map data into the GPS receiver
- Georeferenced maps (that encode each pixel of the image; that is, scanned map, to the real coordinate on the earth's surface, or georeference) that automatically display position coordinates anywhere on the active map; look for maps that allow you to click with your mouse to zoom in on specific segments
- Good product support for future upgrades
- A variety of print and export formats
- The ability to print customized maps
- The ability to upload the trail onto the Internet to share
- E-mail

Optional features you might find with the software include

- Tools for area measurement
- Generate 3-D views of the terrain
- Highlighting or color customization
- Sound and picture attachments to waypoints
- Layered technology allowing map user to customize the level of detail displayed (e.g., one layer is depth contour, one layer is NAVAIDS, one layer is land features)
- FUGAWI, a state-of-the-art program, augments the Kodak digital GPS camera and automatically puts pictures on your maps in the location where the picture was taken

The marine versions feature electronic charts that work with various GPS units. The charts contain essential marine and nautical information found on standard navigation-marine charts with coastline detail: NAVAIDS such as lighthouses, lighted and unlighted buoys, navigation lights, day beacons, and channel markers; spot soundings and depths contours; hazards to navigation; and fixed and floating NAVAIDS. These charts also display radio beacons and drilling platforms, shoreline, and text names. Also included in many areas are obstructions, channels, shipping lanes, restricted areas, pipelines, cables, leading lights, landmarks, anchorages, and other nautical chart features.

You can transfer detailed charts to the GPS receiver quickly, easily, and at a low cost, and with the touch of a button, find the nearest NAVAIDS—regardless of the conditions.

Uploading and Downloading Information

A good e-map set has support programming to interface with most GPS receivers. When you have the proper software installed and your GPS cabled to the serial port on your computer, you can begin. Waypoints and routes can be uploaded into the mapping program and you can customize or document your exact path. This information can be stored and shared with fellow hikers at the click of a mouse.

You'll be able to convert a trail traced on an e-map to a GPS route with waypoints ready for downloading to the GPS unit. Or perhaps you'd like to profile the elevation of the path or hike that you want to take. To access an elevation profile, begin by tracing the trail or road that you'll be taking; the software can generate a cross-sectional view with ascents, descents, total elevation climb, total descending elevation, and minimum and maximum elevations.

Trail guides on CD-ROMs will soon provide waypoints for specific highlights or hikes. You will be able to buy electronic guidebooks that provide CDs containing text, maps, pictures, and GPS routes and waypoints. Web sites (including those of local county and municipal chambers of commerce) will increasingly offer more waypoints and routes to download for free.

Another type of custom map is now available at some USGS offices. In concert with Wildflower Productions, the USGS has kiosks set up in regional offices that can make custom 3-D maps on demand. These digital-map vending machines will become more popular in the future, making the digital-map revolution available for all. A resource list of GPS manufacturers is in the appendix.

—PJC

APPENDIX

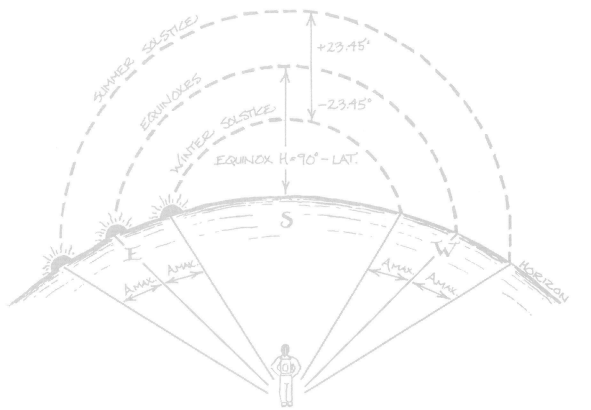

BEARINGS OF SUNRISE AND SUNSET

1. Find the sun's maximum amplitude for your latitude.
2. Scale the north–south baseline of the circular chart for the maximum amplitude on each side of the 0-degree mark.
3. Find today's date along the circumference. Draw a line from the date toward and perpendicular to the baseline. Where the lines intersect is the sun's amplitude for that day at that latitude.
4. To find the sun's bearing when it rises in the Northern Hemisphere, subtract north amplitude from or add south amplitude to 90 degrees (east).
5. To find the sun's bearing when it sets in the Northern Hemisphere, add north amplitude to or subtract south amplitude from 270 degrees (west).

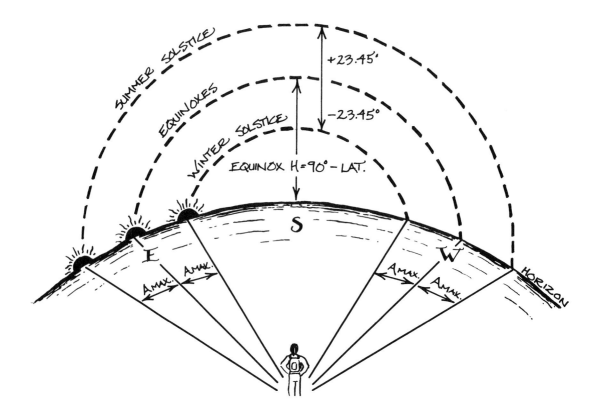

LATITUDE (N or S)	5	10	15	20	25	30	35	40	45	50	55	60
MAXIMUM AMPLITUDE	24°	24°	24°	25°	26°	27°	29°	31°	34°	38°	44°	53°

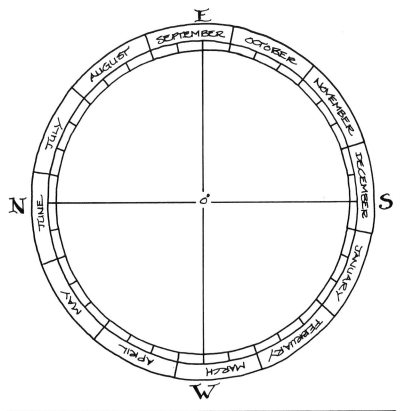

NORTH AMPLITUDES		SOUTH AMPLITUDES	
SUNRISE BEARING	= 90° − AMPLITUDE	SUNRISE BEARING	= 90° + AMPLITUDE
SUNSET BEARING	= 270° + AMPLITUDE	SUNSET BEARING	= 270° − AMPLITUDE

DECLINATION CORRECTIONS

In chapter 3, you learned easy ways to compensate for *declination*, the angular difference between geographic north and magnetic north. However, there may be times when those methods are not available to you, or you may simply prefer the logic of numbers. If so, here is how you can correct for declination.

From Map to Compass

To adjust a direction taken from a map to be used with a compass, do the following:

East declination: subtract. For example, if the direction on a map is 90 degrees and the declination is 12 degrees east, the comparable direction on a compass is 78 degrees.

West declination: add. If the direction on a map is 90 degrees and the declination is 8 degrees west, the comparable direction on a compass is 98 degrees.

From Compass to Map

To adjust a direction taken by a compass to be used on a map, do the following:

East declination: add. If a compass shows a bearing of 90 degrees and the declination is 12 degrees east, the comparable direction on a map is 102 degrees.

West declination: subtract. If a compass shows a bearing of 90 degrees and the declination is 8 degrees west, the comparable direction on a map is 82 degrees.

How to Remember These Rules

There's quite a lot here to recall and, to make it worse, the rules all sound very much alike. Luckily, though, you only need to know the two rules for your particular declination, be it east or west; keep only those in mind and you'll be OK.

West declination: Add from map to compass, subtract from compass to map.

East declination: Add from compass to map, subtract from map to compass.

There's also a mnemonic device that has been used by sailors for the past few centuries and has probably kept a lot of ships off the rocks:

> Declination east, compass least.
> Declination west, compass best.

What this means is that with an east declination, the map reading is greater (best) and the compass reading smaller (least), by the amount of declination. With a west declination, the compass reading is best and the map reading least, by the amount of declination. In each case, you simply add or subtract declination.

Here's one last trick to jump-start your memory. Think of the following saying:

> Empty sea, add water.
> "Empty sea" becomes MTC (Map To Compass). "Add water" becomes add W (west). MTC, add W.

Thus, when converting a bearing from map to compass, add west declination. (Again, declination west, compass best.) From this, you can surmise that you subtract east declination. (Declination east, compass least.) Or, from compass (C) to (T) map (M), you subtract west and add east. If you have more important things to remember, write down this rule for declination in your area (east or west) on the map or glue it on the back of your compass.

Incidentally, when you're describing directions, you won't want to go above 360 degrees. If an addition comes to more than 360 degrees, subtract 360 degrees. For example, if you have to add 20 degrees to 355 degrees, the answer is 375 degrees—minus 360 degrees, which is 15 degrees.

The same 360-degree rule applies to subtraction. If you have to subtract 25 degrees from 15 degrees, begin by borrowing 360 degrees. Add it to the 15 degrees you want to subtract from; then subtract 25 degrees from 375 degrees, and the answer is 350 degrees.

METRIC CONVERSION TABLES

An Act of Congress in 1966 legalized the metric system here in the United States. Almost every other country has gone metric because it is logical and easier to work with, but the United States refuses to change. As a token gesture, USGS topos have a distance scale in kilometers as well as in miles and yards, and U.S. nautical charts have begun a long-term conversion to metric. In almost all other parts of the world, there are only kilometers and meters. So if you're an American citizen carrying a passport, it's a safe bet you'd better learn to think metric. The following conversions might be helpful.

Rough Comparisons

0.4 inch = 1 centimeter,
    or 1 inch = 2.5 centimeters
1 foot = 0.3 meter, or 1 meter = 3¼ feet
39 inches = 1 meter, or 1 yard = 1 meter
⅝ mile = 1 kilometer, or 5 miles = 8 kilometers

Accurate Comparisons

1 millimeter (mm) = 0.039 inch
1 inch = 254 millimeters
1 centimeter (cm) = 0.394 inch
1 inch = 2.54 centimeters
1 foot = 30.48 centimeters
1 foot = 0.305 meter
1 meter (m) = 39.37 inches, or 3.28 feet,
    or 1.09 yards
1 yard = 0.914 meter
1 kilometer (km) = 3,281 feet, or 0.62 mile
1 statute mile = 1.61 kilometers

ORIENTEERING

For some people, being lost isn't enough—they have to make a game of it. If you're one of those people with good map-interpreting and compass skills, and if you think that running (or skiing or snowshoeing in winter) through 2 to 10 miles of backcountry sounds like fun, and if you have a competitive spirit, then you might like to try the sport of orienteering.

Orienteering races are set up so that participants using maps, compasses, and cunning have to find a series of hidden control points in the prescribed order in the least amount of time. The courses are laid out over wooded terrain that is unfamiliar to all contestants. Upon starting, the runner is given a topographical map that is drawn to a large scale and small enough to be held in the hand. Maps can be standard USGS 1:24,000-scale topos, but are more often specially made topo maps at a 1:10,000 scale that are highly detailed and very up-to-date. The top of an orienteering map always represents magnetic (not the usual geographic) north, and vertical MN lines are predrawn so there is no need to bother with declination. (These lines were the reason for the invention of the baseplate compass.) As an additional aid, runners are given a card with a brief written description of each control's location (e.g., "Control #3. At trail junction").

The locations of between five and fifteen orange-and-white control-point markers are circled on the map. The challenge is to quickly orient and interpret the map and then get going toward the first control point as soon as possible. The object is to select the fastest route, which is rarely a straight line; this is where map interpretation comes into play. Is it faster to go over a hill, around it, partway up and follow a contour line, or use a level road that is longer but faster? You have to be able to visualize the best route and then follow it as fast and as accurately as possible. To do this, you have to use all the tricks explained in this book: handrails, catch points, lines and points of reference, aiming off, counting your pace to measure distance covered, and everything else available. Compass work is often crude and fast because taking bearings and plotting them is time-consuming.

After the first control is found, you work your way through all the others. Whoever completes the course in the least time wins. However, the winner is not always the fastest runner. The great equalizer in orienteering is that it is more often wayfinding and mental abilities rather than all-out speed that decide the winner.

There are also less competitive types of orienteering activities offered by some clubs that encourage family participation. These laid-back events are for "wayfarers" or "map-walkers," as they are called within the sport—folks who like a challenge but also want to stop and smell the flowers, watch the birds, or contemplate the meaning of magnetism or other esoterica as they amble along.

Orienteering started in Sweden in the 1920s and still has a large following there. Competitions can attract thousands of runners to an event. The sport was introduced to the United States after World War II and now has a loyal if somewhat more modest following here. Those who get caught up in it can compete on the local, national, and international levels.

If this sounds like something you might want to try, contact the U.S. Orienteering Federation, P.O. Box 1444, Forest Park, GA 30051.

SOURCES OF MAPS, BOOKS, COMPASSES, VIDEOS, GPS MANUFACTURERS, AND ELECTRONIC MAPMAKERS

Maps

Each of the listed federal agencies may carry different types of maps for the area in which you are interested. Online ordering can be quick and painless, but call or e-mail the agency if you have questions, which will be faster than writing a letter. To get the appropriate maps when ordering, be specific about where you will be traveling and the type of maps you need.

The U.S. Geological Survey (USGS) is the government's largest mapping agency, covering almost every inch of the United States, its territories, most national parks, and Antarctica. When you call the U.S. Earth Science Information Center (ESIC), the information and map sales branch of the USGS, they'll help you get the right maps. A good starting point is the free map index for the state in which you'll be traveling (there's a separate one for each state) and the free brochure, *Topographic Map Symbols*; also of interest is *How to Obtain Aerial Photographs*. Maps can be ordered through ESIC or the staff can direct you to a state agency or a local retail outlet. Call ESIC at 888-ASK-USGS (888-275-8747) or visit their Web site, http://ask.usgs.gov. You can also visit the USGS Web site with general information about finding and ordering USGS topographic maps, www.usgs.gov/mac/findmaps.html.

U.S. Federal Agencies

Army Corps of Engineers
U.S. Department of Defense
Office of Public Affairs
441 G St.
Washington DC 20314
202-761-0011
www.usace.army.mil/where.html#maps
Covers navigable inland waterways, lakes, and rivers.

Central Intelligence Agency (CIA)
Office of Public Affairs
Washington DC 20505
703-482-0623
www.cia.gov/cia/publications/mapspub/index.html
More than 100 maps of foreign countries available to the public; not all are useful to wilderness explorers. Ask for *CIA Maps and Publications Released to the Public*.

Earth Resources Observation Systems (EROS)
User Services Section
U.S. Geological Survey
47914 252nd St.
Sioux Falls SD 57198
800-252-4547, 605-594-6151
http://earthexplorer.usgs.gov/
The clearinghouse for federal aerial photographs and space imagery.

National Ocean Service (NOS)
6501 Lafayette Ave.
Riverdale MD 20737
301-436-6990
http://chartmaker.ncd.noaa.gov/
Nautical charts for coastal waters, the Great Lakes, and offshore. Aerial photographs are also available. Charts are available at most boating stores. For a complete description of symbols found on U.S. charts, see *Chart No. 1*.

National Park Service (NPS)
www.nps.gov/parks.html
This links you to a park directory. Once you find the park of your choice, contact it directly to request maps, brochures, and other information.

U.S.D.A. Forest Service (USFS)
Public Affairs Office
National Headquarters
P.O. Box 96090
Washington DC 20090-6090
202-205-1760, ext. 115
http://svinet2.fs.fed.us:80/links/maps/html
Maps for all 155 national forests.

Canadian Government Agencies

Canada Map Office
Geographical Names Section
615 Booth St.
Ottawa ON
Canada K1A 0E9
800-465-6277, 613-952-7000
Fax 800-661-6277
http://maps.nrcan.gc.ca/cmo/dealers.html
Source for the *National Topographic Series* of
    maps that covers all of Canada and its terri-
    tories. Also distributes the Canadian Na-
    tional Parks Maps. Map indexes, price list,
    and brochures on request.

Canadian Hydrographic Service
Department of Fisheries and Oceans
1675 Russell Rd., Box 8080
Ottawa ON
Canada K1G 3H6
613-998-4931
http://chswww.bur.dfo.ca/dfo/chs/
    chs-home.html
Nautical charts of coastal waters, the Great
    Lakes, and major waterways.

Natural Resources Canada Map Office
130 Bentley Ave.
Nepean ON
Canada K1A 0E9

Other Sources

Check the Department of Tourism for the state or
country in which you will be traveling. To find a
good map store near you, contact

International Map Trade Association
P.O. Box 1789
Kankakee IL 60901
815-939-4627
www.maptrade.org

Mail-Order Companies

The following mail-order companies have extensive
stocks of foreign and domestic maps. All the companies are very helpful and can provide maps for
some of the oddest places.

International Travel Maps & Books (ITMB)
    Publishing Ltd.
530 W. Broadway
Vancouver BC
Canada V5Z 4A5
604-879-3621
www.itmb.com

Map Link
30 S. La Patera Ln., Unit #5
Santa Barbara CA 93117
805-692-6777
www.maplink.com

Omni Resources
1004 S. Mebane St.
Burlington NC 27215
800-742-2677
www.omnimap.com

The Map Store
5821 Karric Square Dr.
Dublin OH 43016-4243
800-332-7885
www.themapstore.com

Topo Maps

The following sources provide topographical maps
of the better-known parks and trails.

Adirondack Mountain Club
814 Goggins Rd.
Lake George NY 12845
800-395-8080, 518-668-4447
www.adk.org
Maps for the Adirondack region.

Appalachian Mountain Club
Mail order: Rt. 16, Box 298
Gorham NH 03581
614-523-0636
www.outdoors.org
For the Presidential Range and Maine.

Appalachian Trail Conference
P.O. Box 807
Harpers Ferry WV 25425
304-535-6331
www.appalachiantrail.org
Covers the complete trail through 14 states.

Buckeye Trail Association
P.O. Box 254
Worthington OH 43085
800-881-3062
www.buckeyetrail.org
Maps for the 1,200-mile trail.

Clarkson Map Co.
1225 Delanglade St.
P.O. Box 218
Kaukauna WI 54130
920-766-3000
www.clarksonmap.com
The Canadian Boundary Waters of Minnesota,
    Michigan, and Wisconsin.

Colorado Mountain Club
710 10th St., #200
Golden CO 80401
303-279-3080
www.cmc.org/cmc/
Maps for trails and wilderness areas.

DeLorme Mapping Co.
P.O. Box 298
Yarmouth ME 04096
207-846-7000
www.delorme.com
Topo map atlases of all states.

Earthwalk Press
5432 La Jolla Hermosa Ave.
La Jolla CA 92037
800-828-6277
Covers the parks and wilderness of the West
    and Hawaii.

Finger Lakes Trail Conference
P.O. Box 18048
Rochester NY 14618
716-288-7191
www.fingerlakes.net/trailsystem
Takes you through the 800-mile Finger Lakes
    trail system.

Florida Trail Association
5415 SW 13th St.
P.O. Box 13708
Gainesville FL 32608
800-343-1882
www.florida-trail.org
From South Florida to the Panhandle.

Green Mountain Club
4711 Waterbury–Stowe Rd.
Waterbury Center VT 05677
802-244-7037
www.greenmountainclub.org
Offers maps of the 265-mile Long Trail and
    others.

Green Trails, Inc.
P.O. Box 77734
Seattle WA 98177
206-485-MAPS (206-485-6277)
www.greentrails.com
Maps for the Northwest.

Tom Harrison Cartography
2 Falmouth Cove
San Rafael CA 94901
800-265-9090, 415-456-7940
www.tomharrisonmaps.com
Parks, forests, and wilderness areas of California.

Kingfisher Maps, Inc.
110 Liberty Dr. #100
Clemson SC 29631
800-326-0257, 864-654-2207
www.kingfishermaps.com
Waterproof topographic and bottom-contour
    maps for most lakes east of the Rockies.

New England Cartographics
P.O. Box 9369
N. Amherst MA 01059
888-995-6277, 413-549-4124

www.necartographics.com
Laminated paper maps of the Northeast.

Trails Illustrated
P.O. Box 4357
Evergreen CO 80437
303-670-3457
www.trailsillustrated.com
Waterproof and tearproof maps of most national parks, plus recreational areas in Colorado and Utah. Includes trail descriptions and visitor information. Up-to-date and excellent.

University of Hawaii Press
2840 Kolowalu St.
Honolulu HI 96822
888-UHPRESS (888-847-7377), 808-956-8255
www.uhpress.hawaii.edu
Hawaii and Samoa.

Wilderness Press
1200 5th St.
Berkeley CA 94710
800-443-7227, 510-558-1666
www.wildernesspress.com
Popular hiking areas in California.

Books

Abbey, Edward. *The Journey Home: Some Words in Defense of the American West.* New York: Plume, 1991.

Abbey, Edward. *The Monkey Wrench Gang.* Salt Lake City: Dream Garden Press, 1985.

Burch, David. *Emergency Navigation: Pathfinding Techniques for the Inquisitive and Prudent Mariner.* Camden ME: International Marine, 1986, 1990. The subtitle is modest in its description. Good for sail or power craft on open waters.

Burch, David. *Fundamentals of Kayak Navigation.* Guilford CT: Globe Pequot, 1999. For kayakers and canoeists traveling along the coast; simple, direct, and usable.

Conover, Garrett, and Alexandra Conover. *The Winter Wilderness Companion: Traditional and Native American Skills for the Undiscovered Season.* Camden ME: Ragged Mountain Press, 2001.

Fendler, Donn. *Lost on a Mountain in Maine.* As told to Joseph Egan. New York: Beech Tree Books, 1992. This reprint of the children's classic is still powerful reading.

LaChapelle, Edward R. *The ABC of Avalanche Safety.* Seattle: Mountaineers, 1985.

Leopold, Aldo. *A Sand County Almanac: And Sketches Here and There.* New York: Oxford University Press, 1987, 1989. Another classic now back in print.

Lewis, Meriwether. *The Journals of Lewis and Clark.* Bernard DeVoto, ed. Boston: Houghton Mifflin, 1997. This revised paperback edition brings back into print the abridged journals of the famous expedition. Several other versions are available, but this is my favorite.

Makower, Joel, ed. *The Map Catalog: Every Kind of Map and Chart on Earth and Even Some above It.* New York: Random House, 1993. An excellent resource book on maps, mapmaking, and map usage. Reviews all types of maps (not all of which are appropriate for wilderness use) and where to get them.

McClung, David, and Peter Schaerer. *The Avalanche Handbook.* Seattle: Mountaineers, 1993.

Parry, R. B., and C. R. Perkins, eds. *World Mapping Today.* Boston: Butterworth, 1987. Provides graphic indexes for purchasing currently available maps, usually direct from government sources. International in scope. Need a topo of Swaziland? You'll find it here. General maps as well as topographical, environmental, geological, and others.

Patterson, R. M. *Dangerous River.* Post Mills VT: Chelsea Green, 1990.

Powell, Major John Wesley. *The Exploration of the Colorado River and Its Canyons.* New York: Penguin, 1907.

Townsend, Chris. *The Backpacker's Handbook*, 2nd ed. Camden ME: Ragged Mountain Press, 1997.

Waldron, Malcolm. *Snow Man: John Hornby in the Barren Lands.* New York: Kodansha International, 1998. This classic is back into print as a paperback.

Compasses

Brunton
620 East Monroe Ave.
Riverton WY 82501
800-443-4871, 307-856-6559
www.brunton.com
In addition to the usual variety, it offers its
    patented floating emergency compass: a
    thin, small disk that floats on water.

Silva Compasses
625 Conklin Rd.
Binghamton NY 13902
607-779-2200
www.jwa.com, www.johnsonoutdoors.com/
    camping/silva/index.htm
Very much geared to the sport of orienteering.

Suunto USA
2151 Las Palmas Dr., Suite G
Carlsbad CA 92009
800-543-9124, 760-931-6788
www.suuntousa.com
High quality, limited variety.

Videos

Everyone learns in a different way. If you feel the
message comes across better when seen on TV,
then try these videos.

Brunton
See contact information under Compasses,
    above.
ABC's of Compass and Map, 25 minutes. The
    package includes an instruction pamphlet,
    workbook, the USGS map-symbol guide,
    and a compass.

Quality Video, Inc.
7399 Bush Lake Rd.
Edina MN 55439
*Finding Your Way in the Wild: An Easy Step-by-
    Step Guide to Using a Map and Compass*, 35
    minutes.

GPS Manufacturers

DeLorme
2 DeLorme Dr.
P.O. Box 298
Yarmouth ME 04096
800-452-5931, 207-846-7000
Fax 800-575-2244
www.delorme.com
For use with a laptop computer or Palm-Pilot.

Eagle Electronics
P.O. Box 669
Catoosa OK 74015-0669
800-324-1354
www.eaglegps.com

Garmin International, Inc.
1200 E. 151st St.
Olathe KS 66062 (Kansas City metro area)
913-397-8200
Fax 913-397-8282
www.garmin.com

Lowrance Electronics, Inc.
Tulsa OK 74128-2486
800-324-1356
www.lowrance.com

Magellan Corporation
960 Overland Ct.
San Dimas CA 91773
800-669-4477, 909-394-5000
Fax 909-394-7050
www.magellangps.com

Electronic Mapmakers

A E I
P.O. Box 293
Jemez Springs NM 87025
800-569-1252
www.topo3d.com

Altimap Software
12506 20th Ave. NE
Seattle WA 98125
877-821-4736
www.altimap.com

DeLorme
2 DeLorme Drive
P.O. Box 298
Yarmouth ME 04096
800-452-5931, 207-846-7000
Fax 800-575-2244
www.delorme.com

Hanta Yo Company
521 White Surf Drive
Gaithersburg MD 20878
888-Hanta-Yo (888-426-8296), 301-947-9319
Fax 301-947-9318
www.hantayo.com

iGage/All Topo Maps
1545 S. 1100 E. #3
P.O. Box 58596
Salt Lake City UT 84158-0596
888-450-4922, 801-412-0011
Fax 888-450-4983, 801-412-0022
www.alltopo.com

Maptech, Inc.
1 Riverside Dr.
Andover MA 01810
888-839-5551, 978-933-3000
Fax 978-933-3030
www.maptech.com

Navionics, Inc.
6 Thacher Ln.
Wareham MA 02571
800-848-5896, 508-291-6000
Fax 508-291-6006
www.navionics.com

Nobeltec Corporation
14657 SW Teal Blvd., Suite 132
Beaverton OR 97007
503-579-1414
Fax 503-579-1304
www.nobeltec.com

Northport Systems, Inc.
1246 Yonge St., Suite 302
Toronto ON
Canada M4T 1W5
416-920-0447
Fax 416-964-6313
www.fugawi.com

Wildflower Productions
375 Alabama St., Suite 400
San Francisco CA 94110
415-558-8700
Fax 415-558-9700
www.topo.com

TRAVEL PLAN

Group Members

1. Name:

   Address:

   Who to call in an emergency:

2. Name:

   Address:

   Who to call in an emergency:

3. Name:

   Address:

   Who to call in an emergency:

4. Name:

   Address:

   Who to call in an emergency:

   (Use back of sheet for additional members.)

List visually distinctive equipment:

(continued next page)

(continued from previous page)

Description and location of car(s):

_____

_____

_____

License number(s):

_____

Date and time of departure from trailhead:

_____

Name of trail to be taken:

_____

Describe route (note landmarks, rest and camping sites, objective, return route):

_____

_____

_____

_____

Possible alternate routes:

_____

_____

_____

Estimated date and time of return:

_____

Latest expected return date:

_____

Person(s) to call if overdue or in case of an emergency:

_____

_____

INSTRUCTIONS: Photocopy and fill in this form. Leave completed form with responsible person. Contact this person as soon as you return!

INDEX

nonmapping GPS units, 149
north, finding, 127–29
north, magnetic vs. geographic (true), 51–**52**, **66**–67, 71–73, 86–88. *See also* geographic north; grid north, magnetic north
North Star, **133**, **134**
notes, 113, 117

O

observation skills, 11, 18–19, 56
obstacles, navigating, **80–81**, **83**, **99**
orienteering compasses. *See* baseplate compasses
orienteering (sport), 158
orienting, to external references, 16, 57, 140
orienting compasses
   to geographic north, **71–72**
   to magnetic north, **71**
orienting maps, **56**, 62, 113
Orion, as navigational tool, **136**

P

panic, handling when lost, 122
parallel-channel GPS receivers, 149
passes, on topo maps, **42**
patterns, repeating, as reference line, **17**
patterns, search, **123**
peaks, on topo maps, **42**
pedometers, 106
perspective, 15–16
pilot weed (*Silphium lacinatum*), as directional tool, 126
planimetric maps, 27, **28**
planning
   distances, 106
   local declinations, **66**–67, 156
   routes, 23, 112, **165**–66
   slope profiles, 44–46, **45**
plants, wayfinding lore of, 126
Polaris, as navigational tool
   finding latitude from, **134**
   locating, **133**
Polynesian islanders, navigation system of, 13–14
position
   finding, **54**–57, **100**–102, **107–9**
   returning to, **101**
   tracking a running, 22, 23, 113
positioning, abstract (absolute), 14

positioning, direct (relative), 14
Precision Positioning Service (PPS or P-Code), 148
Principle of Ariadne's Thread, 15, 18
protractors, **53**, 59, 68, 88

Q

quadrangles (quads), on topographic maps, 27, **29**, 31, 32, 48

R

reciprocal bearings. *See* back bearings
reference lines, crossed, **54**–55
reference lines vs. points, 16–18, **17**, **55**, 114. *See also* landmarks
relative vs. absolute positions, 13–14
representation fraction (scale ratio), 48
reverse fixes, **101**
ridges, on topo maps, **42**
rivers, 116, 122
route planning, 18, 106, 112
routes, GPS, 150
ruler, plastic, for maps, 59, 88
running fixes, **102**

S

saddles, on topo maps, **42**
scale, of maps, 32, 48–**49**
senses, developing, 12–14, 18
search patterns, **123**
Selective Availability (SA), 148
sensing direction, 12–14
shaded relief, on maps, 40, **41**
shadows, finding north and south from, **128**
   wayfinding lore, 129
shorebirds, 126
signals, for searchers, 123
sixth sense, 11–13, 18
slope error, 50
slope gradients, 44, **46**
slope profiles, 44–46, **45**
slopes, **42**
small-scale maps, 48–**49**
snow
   navigating in ,142–43
   wayfinding lore, 125, 143
solstices, **130**, **131**

ACKNOWLEDGMENTS

The manuscript for this book was reviewed by Wallace Robbins, longtime Maine forester, professor, and outdoorsman; Chris Townsend, backcountry traveler and author; and Steve Howe, writer/photographer/outdoorsman and Southwest Editor for *Backpacker* magazine. For their valuable insights and criticism, I am indebted. Any remaining inaccuracies or infelicities are mine. I also want to thank Christine Erikson for the fine illustrations she rendered from my crude sketches.

PUBLISHER'S NOTE

Ragged Mountain Press thanks the Brunton Company, of Riverton, Wyoming, and especially Dan Burden, for the loan of several compasses during production of this book.